The Sound of Architecture

Eckhard Gerber

The Sound of Architecture

Eckhard Gerber

Dieter Nellen • Jürgen Tietz • Eds.

jovis

Editorial
Passion and Communication

Dieter Nellen and Jürgen Tietz

The profession of architect can be a lifelong passion. Prominent representatives of the guild, such as Meinhard von Gerkan, Volkwin Marg, Bernhard Winking, Hinnerk Wehberg, and Walter van Lom, are still active late in their life. This also applies to the youngest of them, the Dortmund-based architect Eckhard Gerber. His office, which operates internationally from Dortmund in addition to locations in Hamburg, Berlin, Riyadh, and Shanghai, can now look back on decades of activity, starting in 1966 in Meschede, in Sauerland, under the unassuming name Werkgemeinschaft 66. Today, the office at the firm's headquarters in Dortmund and at other locations worldwide employs approximately 180 people.

Barbara Ettinger-Brinckmann, President of the Bundesarchitektenkammer (Federal Chamber of Architects), celebrated the fiftieth anniversary of Gerber Architekten in 2016: "We freelance architects know what Gerber Architekten has achieved: fifty years of constant work in all of the fields that make our profession so multifaceted and demand constant diligence. Fifty years of conversations with potential clients, fifty years of participating in competitions, fifty years of successes and failures, both of which must be borne, and fifty years of experiences—some of which one could have doubtless done without." Eckhard Gerber and his team have not only designed plans, entered competitions, erected buildings, designed interiors, and dealt with cityscapes and landscapes. The founder and head of the firm to this day, Professor Eckhard Gerber, was equally happy to have his work documented in several publications: at first, through references to various individual projects or ensembles of buildings; and then, in 2013 and 2016, in two encyclopedic books dedicated to his work: *Eckhard Gerber—Baukunst: Bauten und*

Projekte (Eckhard Gerber—architecture: buildings and projects), volumes 1 and 2. And for special purposes of representation, Gerber—a classically educated intellectual—even had two bibliophile editions produced in large format. Another book presenting his work will probably follow, creating a trilogy.

None of this happened simply because of the demands of self-presentation for professional communication that are customary in this line of business, and downright indespensable these days. Rather, it comes from Eckhard Gerber's own intellectual foundation; the joy he takes in narrative and visual discourse; and the aesthetic claim permeating his entire work as an architect, entrepreneur, professor, and human being. Moreover, despite his modest appearance, Gerber is no introvert. He is constantly in dialogue, enjoys a good party (though almost always without any alcohol), and loves friendly conversation and the shared intellectual company of a larger circle. Gerber likes settings that are both sociable and distinguished. And, as one can experience again and again, he is a generous and charming host.

In addition, the communications and media department of his large office is present at international trade fairs and organizes theme- and project-related exhibitions, as well as lecture and discussion events. Good architects produce images, first and foremost architecturally, but also mentally and communicatively. This is how the brand of Gerber Architekten gradually emerged: not as a symbol for architectural seriality with a global signature, but for elegance, authenticity, and individuality in every individual project worldwide. The credo is: "Deriving a design from the specificity of the place, its history, topography, climate, and the surrounding development, as well as a project's energetic, sustainable, and economic dimensions—these are some of the most important parameters of our work. The building—or the urban landscape ensemble—should reflect the genius loci as unique and formulate a striking idea of building and space in the context of all partial aspects" (2018).

A Personal Book: *The Sound of Architecture*

This book is probably the most personal about and by Eckhard Gerber. It is being published under the title *The Sound of Architecture* (*Vom Klang der Architektur*) and thus consciously refers to the important role that music plays in Eckhard Gerber's life, in how he thinks and feels. Gerber himself started making music early on, and he still plays the trumpet today. In addition, his architecture has a musical dimension that combines clarity and emotion. This musical level manifests in the harmony of his compositions of urban space and can be felt in its modulation of spaces and volumes, as one can see in an exemplary way on the campus of the Hochschule für angewandte Wissenschaften Würzburg-Schweinfurt (University of Applied Sciences Würzburg-Schweinfurt), the Westfälische Hochschule Recklinghausen (Recklinghausen Campus of the University of Applied Sciences), or the Niedersächsische Staats- und Universitätsbibliothek (Lower Saxony State and University Library) in Göttingen. And then there is also the special tonality of the materials. All of this together engenders more than just an attitude, more than an architect's signature style. It leads to a special harmony of spaces, structures, and materials in which users move—and which move them.

The Sound of Architecture is, first, the biography of a quintessential German life between east and west, marked by Gerber's childhood in a Protestant pastor's house in Thüringen in East Germany, university studies in Braunschweig in West Germany, and a constant career of being tested on all levels of a demanding profession. It is a biographical essay (with revealing anecdotes) and an assessment and classification of Gerber's work in its contemporary historical context. It offers a stroll—equally enjoyable and informative—through the course of Gerber's architectural career, in the context of German history and postwar culture without which his works would be inconceivable. Traveling with Jürgen Tietz, Gerber undertook two extensive excursions to the most important German sites of his architecture.

In a second part of the book, two long-standing friends, Kaspar Kraemer (Cologne) and Dietrich Sattler (Bremen), political companions such as Gerhard Langemeyer (Dortmund), colleagues such as Jörn Walter (Hamburg), Christa Reicher (Aachen), and Wolfgang Sonne (Dortmund), as well as two publicists, Falk Jaeger and Sebastian Redecke (both from Berlin), each offer personal contributions sharing their own experience and insights in connection with the work of Eckhard Gerber. The art historian Rouven Lotz also agreed to write an essay on the topic of "Art in Architecture."

In this second section, the book addresses the entire spectrum of today's pressing questions for the field: *Baukultur* and the culture of architectural competitions, architecture and urban planning in historical context, the social responsibility of architecture, art in architecture, and the functional and subjective significance of building and landscape. Eckhard Gerber has repeatedly engaged with these important topics as a university teacher and professor and as chairman of countless juries. They are still (the) questions of our time.

Konzept+Atmosphäre: Baukunstarchiv NRW, Dortmund—AIT Architecture Salon Hamburg—Aedes Architecture Forum, Berlin

Gerber lent his support as a patron to the new Baukunstarchiv NRW (Architectural Archive of North Rhine-Westphalia), which opened in 2018—also functioning in some ways as an academy and society for the city and state—even as it was being planned. As a Dortmund architect and citizen of the city, he welcomed a change of use of this kind and rejected the long-standing, politically virulent plans to demolish the site. His own ideas from this period aimed to preserve the historic building and expand its scale. He is not indifferent to the fate of his community; it's a matter that lies close to his heart, as is also true for his professional colleagues Volkwin Marg (from Hamburg) and Christoph Mäckler (from Frankfurt).

In November 2018, the official events celebrating his eightieth birthday took place in the renovated building, together with prominent guests. In 2013, Gerber had already celebrated his seventy-fifth birthday at the same location, and the temporary intervention with its special aesthetics won the city's political leaders over to a plan to give the former museum a (new) future. It was also in 2013 that Gerber Architekten had presented a first exhibition throughout the entire building in order to demonstrate its suitability as a permanent Haus der Architektur (House of Architecture).

Only three weeks after its official opening, the first monographic exhibition about Gerber Architekten, *Konzept+Atmosphäre* (Concept+Atmosphere), was shown in the Baukunstarchiv NRW. The exhibition is documented in this publication. A series of discussions with Reiner Nagel (Bundesstiftung Baukultur), Volkwin Marg, and the Hamburg landscape architect Hinnerk Wehberg accompanied the presentation of the works. From Dortmund, the show will travel to the AIT-ArchitekturSalon in Hamburg and then on to Berlin.

The Sound of Architecture will now be published in the summer of 2019 in conjunction with the closing reception of this series of exhibitions in Germany, which will take place at Aedes in Berlin. What better occasion and better time could there be for publishing an homage to Eckhard Gerber?

The Sound of Architecture
Biographical Notes on Eckhard Gerber

Jürgen Tietz

People are gathering on the stage, walking around slowly, casually. Some are wearing jeans, others are dressed more formally. Music begins, then singing. These are the moments that can't be planned. They are suddenly there, possessing an inner harmony just like this evening in May in the concert hall of the Hochschule für Musik und Theater (University of Music and Theater) in Leipzig, named after the great Felix Mendelssohn Bartholdy. They are moments with a magic that suddenly surrounds you and carries you beyond the present instant. Moments in which sounds and sights and atmosphere deepen and intensify, in which personal and collective history become immediate and palpable.

For two days, we've been making our way through Germany. We're on an initial excursion to get to know old and new projects realized by Eckhard Gerber's office. Of course, we began in Dortmund. Early in the morning, Professor Gerber picks me up directly across from what used to be the Landesbank, designed by Harald Deilmann, which is just now beginning a second life as a historically protected monument of late modernism. We will find time to discuss Deilmann, who represents an important personal and architectural reference point in Gerber's early years.

Our trip through Germany will take us via the Riedberg campus of the Goethe Universität in Frankfurt am Main to the Neue Messe Karlsruhe (Karlsruhe Trade Fair and Exhibition Center). With its clear structure and striking, cantilevered canopy, it is one of those core buildings in Gerber's oeuvre in which function and aesthetics, modernity and timelessness, vividly align. From there, our journey will head out again across the countryside, all the way to Würzburg.

As we drive along the *Autobahn,* a conversation begins that revolves in ever wider arcs around Gerber's biography, his education and his architecture. Slowly at first, the exchange finally gets going and develops into conversations about buildings and competitions, competition juries, and above all people. About Günter Behnisch, for instance, whose body of successful architectural work fascinates Gerber, himself a staunch proponent of modernism. And from Behnisch's works, nothing fascinates Gerber more than the Olympic Stadium Behnisch designed in Munich: "Behnisch built open structures, which I found interesting because this approach to architecture offered a future, because it was something that could be expanded on." Early in his career, Gerber sought contact with Behnisch, who was a good fifteen years his senior. "I always kept an eye on Behnisch and later met him many times because I was interested in everything he did, both as an architect and as a businessman." Gerber first met Behnisch together with the architect Jörg Friedrich, from Hamburg, after a competition for an education center for lawyers in Recklinghausen in which Gerber himself took second place. Behnisch was so impressed by his younger colleague's design that he called Gerber to congratulate him on the extraordinary work. In the years that followed, Friedrich developed into an accomplished university architect and designer of theater spaces. For example, in Erfurt: in 1997, Gerber was appointed to sit on the prize jury for a new building chaired by the tremendously eloquent architect Max Bächer, together with Carlo Weber, who had been Behnisch's partner. Friedrich won the competition, and his design was also built, albeit at a different location than initially planned. Gerber remained in contact with Weber (who opened a firm of his own together with Fritz Auer in Munich and Stuttgart in 1980, after many years of working with Behnisch) until Weber's death in 2014. Architecture is always personal—for those who use it and connect it to their own experiences and stories, for all who initiate it and finance it, and of course for the architects who design buildings or shepherd them through an architectural competition.

In Würzburg, we visit another university, the beautiful home of the Hochschule für angewandte Wissenschaften Würzburg-Schweinfurt (University of Applied Sciences of Würzburg-Schweinfurt), built in 2011. It will not be the last university campus we explore on our travels. We will find time to visit the Recklinghausen campus of the Westfälische Hochschule in Recklinghausen (University of Applied Sciences in Westphalia), for example—which in the 1990s functioned like an initial spark for the buildings that

Gerber then began to realize for educational organizations and institutes. Or the compact brick cube of the Aus- und Fortbildungszentrums für Brauerei (Training and Research Center for the Institute for Brewing) in the Berlin district of Wedding, with its sculptural staircases grouped around a spacious hall designed to be flooded with light.

Today, buildings for educational institutions are one of the focal points of Gerber's extensive work, which encompasses around 250 completed projects. The campus of the Hochschule für angewandte Wissenschaften (University of Applied Sciences) lies, concrete-clear, on a slope just outside the city. Two L-shaped buildings of different heights protectively enclose an inner campus square. A glass façade, given rhythm by green opening elements, responds to the prefabricated concrete elements colored like the sand from the River Main. Here, Gerber has worked sensitively with the landscape, creating a harmoniously modulated ensemble that is integral and unified, but not hermetically so. From the building, one's gaze can meander along the gentle, moving slopes that descend toward the Main. This is one aspect that runs through Gerber's work as a leitmotif: his precise way of seeing the potential a location holds, and the possibilities that topography offers to architecture. A pyramid-shaped outdoor staircase leads from the campus in Würzburg down to a meadow with orchards. With a friendly wink, it reminds you of Alvar Aalto's famous grass-covered outer staircase for the town house he built in 1952 in Säynätsalo, Finland. My sense is that Aalto, too, will be a topic of our discussions, as a significant figure whose influence on all the architects who studied in Germany in the 1950s and early 1960s can hardly be overestimated. The formative power of Aalto's work ranges from construction tasks to the language of form and materiality, the concept of space itself, and the intensive relationship between architecture and landscape.

The next day, two more major works of Gerber are on the itinerary: the Landesfunkhaus Sachsen-Anhalt des MDR (MDR Regional Radio Broadcasting Center in Magdeburg, 1998) and the Universitätsbibliothek (University Library) in Göttingen, which opened in 1993 after a long period of planning. This will be followed by additional tours through Germany. These journeys will take us to the Sauerland, to the city of Meschede, where Gerber took his first steps toward independence as a freelance architect, and of course through Dortmund, where he has had close ties for almost forty years.

Concert hall of the Hochschule für Musik und Theater "Felix Mendelssohn Bartholdy," Leipzig, competition first prize, 1995•2001

Concert hall of the Hochschule für Musik und Theater "Felix Mendelssohn Bartholdy," Leipzig, competition first prize, 1995•2001

But First, Leipzig

Slowly, evening descends over the city, known for its international trade fairs, as we reach the music district outside the old city center. It's a special district, and not only because of its buildings from the *Gründerzeit,* the period of economic expansion following Germany's unification in 1871. This is where Clara and Robert Schumann and Felix Mendelssohn Bartholdy made European music history as key figures of Romanticism. And where internationally renowned conductors such as Arthur Nikisch, Wilhelm Furtwängler, and Bruno Walter left their mark. Our main intention was only to look at the structure designed by Gerber, which adjoins the old *Gründerzeit* building like a wooden casket, or perhaps even like an autonomous resonating body made of wood. Hopefully, we won't interrupt the rehearsal that is scheduled to begin shortly. There is only a week left before the students will perform Mozart's *Don Giovanni* in the hall, which holds an audience of 400.

As in Würzburg, Gerber also realized an L-shaped building in Leipzig: a slender wing facing the street, elevated and narrow, provides space for the artists' dressing rooms, ancillary rooms, and a series of practice rooms for music students, with glass walls toward the inner courtyard, which has been designed in harmony with the older building. Like most of Gerber's projects, this was a winning entry in a competition. His older daughter Nicola played a major role in designing the competition and then worked with Jens Haake on further project planning. The main wing, however, is the concert hall, which opened in 2001. Inside and outside, it is largely clad in wood, and on the ground floor it opens with generous glass structures toward the charming inner courtyard, where it affords a glimpse back into the hall itself. A glass joint connects the old building made of stone and the new building clad in honey-colored timber. Beneath this element, one finds a small foyer through which the concrete control booth on the upper floor extends diagonally into the old building. Inscribed upon it are the names of all the donors who contributed to the construction of the new concert hall, as a thank you from the university. A feeling of joyful excitement prevails in the gently rising orchestra seats. People stream in and out of the doors to the side foyer. Coats and bags are scattered across the black seats; people are starting to sit, chatting and laughing. Quietly, we take a seat in the gallery. From here, we have a view of the orchestra pit and the stage, where we see the dark set on a red floor and, on three panels, the contours of a naked, recumbent woman. An obvious choice, since the set is for the womanizer Don Giovanni.

Behind the set, the hall has a large organ that is nevertheless out of sight, covered up. For acoustic reasons, the wooden paneling stretches along the side walls of the hall like waves, and it is no coincidence that, once again, I must think of Alvar Aalto's architecture. Amid the chatter, the rehearsal suddenly begins. Matthias Foremny enters the room, the doors are closed, the space falls silent, the piece begins and is immediately interrupted again for corrections, and then the singing continues. Foremny announces the bars that are to be rehearsed, and we, the audience, are drawn away into Mozart's world. Sound and space merge into a world of their own, as if the earth were to devour us as it does Don Giovanni at the end of the opera. But after almost two hours of rehearsal, we are released and free to go, enchanted and fascinated. We are able to speak briefly with Foremny before he leaves for the weekend, and we make sure to praise the production, to note what a demanding piece *Don Giovanni* is and how remarkable his students are.

My head is buzzing after so much sound and so much architecture. And yet it is in Leipzig that I have gained a clearer idea of what Eckhard Gerber's architecture is all about. It is shaped in equal measure by the strict rationality and feeling for music that have accompanied him throughout his life as a musician who plays the jazz trumpet. He modestly corrects me when I later ask him about this: "I'm not a musician, I just like to play," he says. And yet: for me it was a special moment to experience the rehearsals for *Don Giovanni* at Gerber's music school in Leipzig. The combination was marvelous, even magical. Gerber smiles at my choice of words, but he knows that these are the two dimensions that give his work form and strength: one is analytic, the other inspired by the muses, free, artistic. We repeatedly encounter both in Gerber's work—and always in new variations.

Eckhard Gerber with his mother,
Emmy Gerber, 1943

Roots in Thuringia

The Protestant pastor's house is a topos of German cultural history, and you can experience its archetype in the Bugenhagenhaus in Lutherstadt Wittenberg. This is where the confidant of the reformer Martin Luther, Johannes Bugenhagen, lived and worked. Beginning in 1532, Bugenhagen was the pastor for the main congregation in Wittenberg. One can hardly overstate the influence that the Protestant worldview of faith and duty subsequently came to hold over large parts of northern and central Germany. Hence, it's not surprising that this influence extended to the area's architects, as well. Like Volkwin Marg, Gerber's friend from his Braunschweig university days, who is also the founding partner of the Hamburg-based firm Architects von Gerkan, Marg and Partners, Gerber's biography is rooted in a Protestant parsonage. Curiously enough for both men, this was in East Germany, and both men were deeply shaped by this origin. Is it a coincidence that Gerber completed his degree in 1966 at the TU Braunschweig under Friedrich Wilhelm Kraemer with a design for a church center, including a church, kindergarten, and nursing home?

Eckhard Gerber was born in 1938 in Oberhain as the third of six children. Oberhain lies in the Thuringian Forest, about fifty kilometers south of Erfurt. The final syllable "-hard" in his first name is something he shares with his brothers Eberhard (1935), Gotthard (1937), Eckhard (1938), Volkhard (1941) and Manhard (1945), while his sister, born in 1949, was named Mechthild. When his sister was born, the pastor's family had already been living in Großenlupnitz near the Lutherstadt Eisenach for eight years. Gerber's father Hans came from a family rooted in Thuringia, but he himself was born in 1906 in Bromberg (today Bydgoszcz, Poland) and later attended school in Eisenach. Gerber's mother, born in 1912, came from a pastor's family. The fact that Eckhard Gerber's grandfather, Günter Scheibe, belonged to the Confessing Church during the Third Reich, which resisted government efforts to coopt religious institutions, while his father was close to the German Christians, who were associated with the National Socialists and whose main church was the Dresden Frauenkirche, caused tensions within the family that the young Eckhard was of course not able to understand at the time. His own assessment is that the clarity and structure of Protestant thought and action with which he grew up played an important role in his later development. This also applied to the clear spatial and social structures of his childhood. "With its high tower and square, the church formed the center of the village. Socially, everything was also clearly structured: there

Parsonage in Oberhain, where Eckhard Gerber was born

Eckhard Gerber in Oberhain, 1939

Eckhard Gerber at his aunt's Ise in Schmalkalden, 1942

Parents Hans and Emmy Gerber with their children (*from left*) Eberhard, Gotthard, Volkhard, and Eckhard, Großenlupnitz, 1942

Parents Hans and Emmy Gerber with all their children (*from left to right*) Eberhard, Volkhard, Gotthard, Eckhard, Mechthild, and Manhard, Großheringen, 1955

were three important people—the priest, the teacher, and the mayor." This clarity also characterized the Gerber family structure: the father was rather strict, but always concerned about the welfare of his children. "Everyone had to graduate from high school, there was no discussion to be had about that. And [my father] always had a very clear intention, especially when it came to the education of his children and their upbringing according to principles of Christian ethics: 'decent behavior,' for example, was a frequent phrase for admonishing the children." Gerber's mother, by contrast, was loving and sensitive, the go-to person for matters large and small.

In addition to a stuffed animal, one of the earliest images that Gerber remembers from his childhood is the house where he was born: a black-gray slate building with two front doors, arranged symmetrically along its axis to the right and left at the ends of the main façade. "An image that has somehow stayed with me my whole life," he notes in his memoirs. The same sense of order was found in the structure of the village Oberhain, with its ascending village street lined on both sides by slate houses. The high church tower and the church nave formed the end of the street. And yet there were also the smells of childhood, for example, in the house of his godmother, where he remembers the odor of stables and cows, "because stables and our living quarters were combined here under one roof." Not to mention the delicious Thuringian dumplings, with plenty of sauce and meat. Gerber's childhood years in the idyllic village of Großenlupnitz, where the family lived in the parsonage on a small side street of Hauptdorfstraße, were formative for him. Here, too, the house included barns and stables grouped around a courtyard. Behind these, there was the garden and a meadow, bordered by the small river Böber.

Less pleasant for the Gerber boys was the feeling, as pastor's children, of constantly being monitored by the villagers. The world in which Eckhard Gerber grew up was not only clearly structured. It was a small world with strict conventions and rules, which of course included Sunday church attendance. Gerber's inclination for music, which is still with him today, is rooted in his childhood. His oldest brother learned piano, the second oldest, violin. This left Gerber with the recorder, allowing the family to perform small concerts in the house. Attending a music lesson meant walking for an hour to reach Eisenach. Together with his siblings and his mother, he sang in the church choir, which performed on church holidays as well as at weddings, baptisms, and funerals. Choir rehearsals took place in the evenings in the confirmation room of the parsonage. These were always a special experience, for the stories

Großenlupnitz with church

Village street in Großenlupnitz

that the adults told among themselves there were tremendously exciting for the children and young people.

Gerber intuitively absorbed the spatial structure of the village and internalized it. It thus became a leitmotif for his later work as an architect. Like Oberhain, Großenlupnitz—where the family had lived since 1941—was also characterized by an ascending village street, ending at a dominating church with its bell tower. "For my whole life, this image has shaped me as a symbol of structure, order, and hierarchy." On both sides of the village road, farmers had their homes and courtyards. Usually, these were arranged together as a gabled house and a barn, also gabled, with a larger gate in between. Behind them was the courtyard, closed off on the other side by another barn. "Both this U-shaped structure, open toward the street but with a threshold defined by the gate, and the permeability of the barn to the open landscape behind it, made a deep, natural imprint on me that often returned in my later buildings and designs." We were particularly successful with construction projects in which the building was formulated as a link or transition from the built space of the village or city to the open landscape. This is how we won many competitions."

Anyone who engages with the numerous buildings that Eckhard Gerber has constructed over the past fifty years will soon realize that they are not shaped by any specific architectural signature they might impose upon a location. Rather, despite their geometric clarity, his buildings are characterized by a deeper understanding of each respective location and its potential. His designs thus create spatial landscapes in which the building and its surroundings are conceived and rhythmized cohesively in context with each other. Gerber's creativity springs on the one hand from his experience as an architect, on the other from the well of the unconscious deeply anchored in our memories, a source we collect and carry with us, over the years and decades, in our own personal store of sense impressions and spatial experiences.

Life in Großenlupnitz was simple, rural. From today's point of view, it seems almost archaic. Water came from a spring well, through pipes that led to the buildings. The water pressure, however, only reached the ground floor. The farmers used the village well, also fed by the spring water, to cool their large milk cans. In the morning, these cans were taken to a collection point and picked up by the milk truck, which then took them to the dairy. In the early afternoon, the truck came back with the empty milk cans, some of them filled with whey. "Since we were often hungry during the war, we paid close attention to when the jugs from the dairy were returned to where they had been collected so that we could bring them to the farmers. In return, the farmers gave us a nice piece of bread with lard or liverwurst. Of course, we only took the cans of farmers who we knew would give us something. The cans of the stingy farmers were left standing on the rack where they had been delivered."

The young boy spent a lot of time in the village's small carpentry workshop and wood turnery. He enjoyed the wonderful smell of wood and occasionally helped to build wooden constructions. He watched, for example, to see how table legs, spinning wheels, or wooden wagon wheels were made. The large metal outer rings and small metal rings on the middle hubs were made by the village blacksmith: "They were made so hot that they would shrink as they cooled and stabilize the wheel with their pressure." The forge was also where the horses were shod. The boy was particularly fascinated by the furnace, which was supplied with oxygen by a hand-operated bellows, later by an electric motor, until the coal made the iron glow, allowing it to be forged with hammer and anvil. "As a little boy, I was connected with craftsmanship from the very beginning," Gerber remembers. "To me, everything that happened in the workshops was reasonable, self-evident, and comprehensible."

The course of the year from spring through summer, autumn, and winter was not only represented by sun, rain, snow, and frozen brooks and ponds, but above all in the course of the agricultural year. This ranged from sowing in spring to picking beets and harvesting grain, which at the time was still done by scythe. "As a boy, I already knew how important it was to make sure that the straw and the feeding hay were not stored when they were damp, because otherwise a fire could develop, which did sometimes happen in the villages."

Gerber's descriptions of this archaic rural labor remind one of Edgar Reitz's television series *Heimat,* which means "home" or "homeland"—a seemingly distant time that is not actually so far in the past. Gerber watched with curiosity as the threshed grain was transported to the mill in Großenlupnitz on the Nesse River, a small tributary of the Werra River near Eisenach. The water provided the power to operate the mill: "There was a weir that dammed up the water, and over which the excess water was diverted. I could see quite clearly how the water wheel of the mill was driven by the water as it was dammed up, to then be pushed, falling, through a side channel; and how, in the mill itself, to which we had frequent access, the rotating axle transferred this force to the machinery and from there to the mill wheels. What we found especially interesting was the elevator, a kind of lifting platform, that allowed us to go up or down by pulling on a rope." This accessibility to the individual floors was necessary because the production process of the grinding took place vertically from top to bottom, and one always had to physically go to each area to carry out checks."

His father's parsonage included a small plot of land. Especially during the war and postwar years, this is where the family kept chickens, ducks, geese, and rabbits for the Sunday roast, together with two pigs and a few goats and sheep. "The sheep went out during the day with a shepherd who collected them from all the villagers in the morning, leading a flock that grew and grew as he moved through the village into the surrounding meadows and pastures. He whistled as he came through the streets and alleys. We would open our gate and our sheep would join the flock. All of the sheep had corresponding marks so that everyone could see whose was whose. And in the evening, the shepherd would come back through the village with the flock. We would open our gate and our sheep would push themselves to the side of the flock ten or fifteen meters before they reached it so that they could then quite easily come into our yard. In other words, they knew exactly where they lived. It was only once in a while that one of the sheep was caught daydreaming, which we then had to quickly fish out of the flock."

Despite the dangers and deprivations of the war and the postwar years, this sounds like an idyllic childhood, one in which the brothers often frolicked around together in the open countryside But the boys also had to work in the yard and the garden. There were fences to repair and a chicken coop that had to be built. Together with his father, Gerber built their first apiary in Großenlupnitz: "Nails had to be made from steel wire, and planks, boards, or slats (to be used as posts) were sawed, sharpened, nailed, and set straight with a spirit level or plumb line." But one evening in the middle of the Second World War, it became clear just how threatened and fragile this childhood idyll was. Gerber remembers how his father took him together with his brothers and sisters up a small hill at the end of the village in the direction of Eisenach to show them the glowing red sky. "It was no sunset but rather the red glow of Kassel as it burned, about a hundred kilometers away." On October 22, 1943, the bombardment sparked a firestorm that completely destroyed the old town with its half-timbered houses. For Gerber, anxious memories also come from the bombings of nearby Eisenach, which the family fled, heading to the cellar of the parsonage, and from his encounter with the gigantic steel tanks.

As the only pastor left in the entire region, his father served twelve churches and parishes at that time. With his Ford Eifel, purchased many years earlier

The Wartburg near Eisenach

Parsonage in Großenlupnitz
with Eckhard Gerber, his daughter,
Gesche, and his brother,
Eberhard, ca. 1993

in 1934, he drove to the various villages for church services, often taking his children with him. At the end of the war, shortly before American troops occupied Thuringia, the parsonage in Großenlupnitz took on even more inhabitants, providing shelter to his mother's sister, husband, children, and father-in-law, who had been forced to flee the Eastern territories. Caring for so many people became a challenge for his mother; food was rationed with food stamps: "I remember that my mother used to send me to the bakery to get buns. I gave the baker stamps for ten buns, telling her: 'I'd like twelve buns.' She looked at the stamps, looked at me, and gave me the twelve buns. I ate one of the extras right away, and proudly returned home with the other." Shortly before the end of the Second World War, two SS men with pistols forced Gerber's father to hand over his Ford Eifel, probably so that they could escape quickly. Since the father was quite attached to his car, he asked the men to promise that they would return it to him after the end of the war. "Of course, he never saw it again. Much later he found out that it had been left—plundered, without wheels and completely scrapped—somewhere near Eisenach." During this time, shortly before the end of the war, other things happened that could have been life-threatening for the entire family. The father hid a deserted soldier in the attic of the parsonage: a man who would later become the director of the world-famous Thomanerchor in Leipzig. This man remained a friend of the family his entire life, and like Gerber's father, he had sympathies with the German Christians, the movement within the German Protestant Church that sought to align the church with Nazi ideology.

For Eckhard Gerber, the end of the war in May 1945 was accompanied by the beginning of his schooling in the fall. The path to school was short, since the school was right next to the church. "Of course, I was familiar with this classroom, and my greatest concern was remembering my assigned place among so many other students. This was a worry that turned out not to be necessary at all."

As was usual at the time, several classes were taught at the same time in one classroom. The experienced village school teacher personally knew not only the children of the four cohorts gathered in this one class, but also their parents and grandparents. The good students were encouraged just as those who weren't so good; the latter improved their performance by constantly practicing the basics. But the education in the elementary school was increasingly dominated by the communist ideology of teachers who became more and more loyal to party principles. By mid-1945, the Americans had already withdrawn from Thuringia, leaving it to the Red Army in exchange for West Berlin, as was decided at the Yalta Conference. This was not a good situation for the Gerber siblings: "As pastor's children, we didn't fit into this system." Naturally, that also applied to Gerber's father: "As village pastor, he had been at the center of public life. Now he was declared to be an unwanted opponent of the system because he was a pastor." This directly affected the children. Eckhard Gerber's eldest brother Eberhard was not allowed to attend high school in what was then the eastern zone or to earn a high school degree. This was an unimaginable situation for Hans Gerber. In 1949, the year the two German states were founded, he thus took his son Eberhard across the unfenced "green border" between the occupation zones. "Together with a friend who was also a pastor, my father accompanied my brother at night to the forest near Obersuhl. From there, he showed him a house that was already in the West and where people were waiting for him." Eberhard ultimately graduated from high school at the Melanchthon School in Steinatal near Kassel, financially supported by the family's Western relatives. Eckhard sorely missed his big brother. It wasn't until the mid-fifties that the two were able to meet again. Gerber's second brother, Gotthard, however, was lucky. He was allowed to attend high school in Eisenach.

When the American troops left, Hans Gerber took the precaution of marking the pastor's house with a sign in Russian declaring it a "Protestant parsonage," with the hope this would protect it from intrusions by the Russian soldiers stationed nearby, which were frequent at first. He also billeted a Russian officer with the family. The hope was that this would also provide protection against the Russians, who had the reputation of being unpredictable. But the children developed a good relationship with the Russian officer, who would usually head out at night with his stolen car. "He came home in the morning with all kinds of things he had stolen, which he kept in several boxes. During the day he was busy helping us at home, sawing and chopping wood." When the children helped him, he rewarded them with food.

Despite these positive experiences, the residents of Großenlupnitz lived in renewed fear of the Communist occupation, a fear that had initially abated with the end of the war and the American occupation. "I learned that creating fear serves a system for bringing people under control. This marked me deeply, giving me the will to fight back against these fears and not accept them as such myself. I still remember a situation when a policeman came into our house and confronted my father, in a matter that also related to me. I had lost my ID, in which was hidden a five D-mark note that I had received from the West for my birthday in a letter from my godmother. This was apparently a terrible offense and led, of course, to the confiscation of the money. It made me very sad, but also angry," Gerber says, remembering his first conflict with the unjust East German regime.

In 1951, the Gerber family left Großenlupnitz. Hans Gerber accepted a new post as pastor in Großheringen, which lies between Naumburg and Apolda where the River Ilm joins the Saale. That is where Eckhard Gerber met Dietrich Sattler, a friend for life. As editor of the works of Friedrich Hölderlin in the Stroemfeld/Roter Stern Publishing House, Sattler would later make a great contribution to Hölderlin's reception and to German literature overall. At the beginning of the 1950s, however, the children living next door simply played happily together and shared two intensive years of adolescence, in which they talked a lot with each other, built shacks in the woods, went fishing, and took bicycle tours and Sunday hikes to the Rudelsburg castle ruins or to Saaleck Castle and the country inn Himmelreich, or Heavenly Kingdom, that still lies directly across from the castle on the other side of a large bend in the river. This setting is among the unique landscapes where the Saale river has cut its way deep into the limestone rock, and the castles rise out of the jagged cliffs like geometrical structures—another of Eckhard Gerber's lasting memories.

Another significant influence on Gerber was his class teacher, Herbert Hensel, who taught the boys German, mathematics, and art. "It was a good mixture of the most important subjects for my later studies, although this was something of which I had no idea at the time." Together with Hensel, a former Wehrmacht officer who needed recognition in the East German system in order to prove his party loyalty, Gerber initiated traveling exhibitions that Hensel conceived with the two boys. Wall panels were created for exhibitions on the Wartburg Festival, the festival at Hambach Castle, the Korean War, and German-Soviet friendship. "For the boards, we made drawings and texts and created the layout. Everything had to be perfect and graphically well designed. This was of great importance to Herbert Hensel, a painter, excellent teacher, and strategist who always gave precise instructions. It was Dietrich, though, who proved to be the better draftsman and signwriter," Gerber recalls.

In addition to school and his work in the field and garden, Gerber also took up other crafts. Once again, he built an apiary as well as a stable for sheep and goats. Architectural, spatial thinking was something he immediately grasped—with unexpected consequences, as he recalls in retrospect: "Once

Rudelsburg castle and Saaleck
castle near Großheringen

Church in Großheringen

Sand castle in Kühlungsborn with Rudelsburg castle and Saaleck castle, built by Eckhard Gerber and Dietrich Sattler, 1952

Eckhard Gerber (*left*) and Dietrich Sattler (*right*) in Kühlungsborn, 1952

Eckhard Gerber building the sand castle

in a mathematics class, there was a nasty disagreement between my teacher, Mr. Hensel, and me. He drew us a square on the blackboard with the sides A. Next to that, he drew a parallelogram that also had the same side lengths as A and asked me whether this parallelogram had the same area as the square. Of course, I answered yes, and when he drew another parallelogram next to the first, which had even more acute angles, and asked me once again whether this had the same square area, I answered yes again with firm certainty. He got very angry because he thought I was intentionally trying to annoy him. But that wasn't my intention at all. Rather, I saw this parallelogram as a square drawn in perspective, i.e., as a square with the same surface, only foreshortened. Unfortunately, this moment between a student and his teacher made it impossible to explain this to him, which is something I still feel sorry about today."

The introduction of agricultural production cooperatives to the GDR, the *Landwirtschaftliche Produktionsgenossenschaften* or LPGs, prompted the Sattlers to decide to flee from their farm in the spring of 1953 in order to escape terror or arrest by the GDR regime. It was simply impossible to earn enough to cover the excessively high taxes on agricultural products that the state was imposing, and the consequence was a threat of being charged with sabotage. The inner border between the two German states had long since been closed, but it was still possible to flee via Berlin. Dietrich Sattler confided in his friend and told him about the family's secret plan: "I was the only one Dietrich told about the planned escape, two days before it was to happen, and of course only in the strictest secrecy. Until then, I had witnessed the Sattlers' terrible fears and helplessness. It takes a lot for a family to leave their farm and their home and set out into the unknown with only a suitcase."

The growing repression of the regime in East Berlin, which was ultimately controlled by Moscow, affected the Gerbers, too. Although Eckhard Gerber was the best in his class, he—like his eldest brother—faced the threat of not being able to attend high school because he was not a "child of workers and farmers." A solution came unexpectedly, as a consequence of the extremely tense political situation in the GDR that followed the popular uprising of June 17, 1953, which coincided exactly with the completion of Gerber's eight years in elementary school, or *Volksschule.* "In order to counteract the uprising against the system, the GDR government instituted measures that included at least a temporary lifting of these restrictions on the children of 'intellectuals' accessing education, which allowed me to then go to secondary school." Together with his brother Gotthard, he attended the

Geschwister-Scholl-Oberschule (Hans and Sophie Scholl High School) in Apolda. The path to school from the Apolda train station led past Egon Eiermann's factory building. The old brick building, in conjunction with its modern concrete skeleton construction, made a deep impression on the boy who would later become an architect, even though he at that time knew nothing about Egon Eiermann. What mattered to Gerber in those days was that he belonged to the Junge Gemeinde (Young Community), the oppositional group of young Christians in the GDR, and not to the party-line Junge Pioniere (Young Pioneers) or the Freie Deutsche Jugend (Free German Youth), which were the official youth organizations of the SED.

As in Großenlupnitz, music was an important constant in Gerber's life in Großheringen. He now received piano lessons, though it turned out this instrument didn't really suit him. He got much more excited about the old trumpet that his brother Eberhard had brought back from the "golden West." The Western trumpet remained in the East, while Eberhard bought a new, much-cheaper instrument in the GDR for his school band's trumpet player. With the old trumpet, a new passion began for Eckhard Gerber, one which continues to the present day. "In no time at all I was able to play a wide variety of pieces; I found myself drawn toward the muse of levity and managed to get sheet music for hit pop songs. Only four weeks later, I had a gig with a band that played in Großheringen and Bad Sulza." Gerber also became the trumpeter for the Vogtscombo, or Bailiff's Combo, the jazz band of the Geschwister-Scholl-Oberschule, where he attended school beginning in autumn 1953. The band consisted of piano, guitar, bass, drums, trumpet, trombone, and clarinet as well as a saxophone played by the pianist Hanno Rempel, a boy who was a year younger but attended the same school. "We wanted to play jazz and the new songs 'from the West,' for which, of course, there was no sheet music in the GDR. But that wasn't a problem for Hanno. He listened to the music on the radio station RIAS and then wrote down the notes—not only the melody, but also the parts for each instrument, including the original chords, so that we could practice the pieces. We then played the music at all kinds of events, from dance class parties to village festivals, which were organized from time to time by local schools and classified as a 'social activity.' This, of course, often led to problems. The atmosphere in the hall regularly got out of hand; people sometimes ended up dancing on the tables and benches. More than once, the band was ordered to appear in the school director's office—a committed GDR Communist who reprimanded us for the music we played and

Ludwig Müller (trombone), Eckhard Gerber (trumpet), members of the Vogtscombo (Bailiff's Combo), a school band in Apolda, and Gotthard Gerber (trombone), while he was studying liturgical music, Großheringen, 1956

the clothes we wore. In the later years of our studies, we often played jazz concerts and took part in competitions."

Music, especially jazz, developed into a leitmotif for Gerber. This became obvious not only from the evening we spent together at the Hochschule für Musik und Theater in Leipzig. It is manifest in his architectural oeuvre, which moves between the poles of strict structure with clear geometries and a musical poetry full of emotion: "In playing jazz, I especially loved the freedom of musical expression. In jazz, the theme defined by the piece, the structure, and the underlying chord progressions provide an opportunity for free improvisation. Improvisation takes place within the framework of these chord progressions, but you are completely free to invent new arrangements. What I like best is playing a melodic instrument. It sets the tone, it is the leading instrument. And yet it still allows you to move around within the shared social space of the band by improvising within the chord progressions. This is completely different with a harmonic instrument like the piano or the guitar. They provide the basis for the chord progressions and guide the rhythm. Music became one of my most important hobbies, which also led to beautiful lifelong friendships. Songs like "I Can't Give You Anything but Love" or "When the Saints Go Marching In" or "Lady Be Good" were jazz standards that everyone always liked to hear and that kept running through your head even without a trumpet—always in search of new melodic variations or phrases for improvisation. Each piece had a fixed concept in the sequence of refrain and improvisation, with an arrangement that we had practiced. We often figured out the improvisational parts while we were playing by responding to the audience." But we also had jazz sessions with other musicians where everything was open, and the pieces we knew well always worked out anyway.

Gerber won over his father, who was more than a bit reticent about this new passion, by accompanying the church chorales on Sundays. He was supported by his brother Gotthard, who, in the meantime, had started to play the organ in addition to the violin. For Gotthard Gerber, this passion became his profession. Initially, he studied liturgical music and organ at the Church Music School in Eisenach with Erhard Mauersberger, the family friend who would later become the conductor of the Thomankerchor in Leipzig. Later, Gotthard attended the conservatory in Frankfurt am Main, where he studied with Helmut Walcha.

A New Orientation

At school, Eckhard Gerber was forced to develop his very own form of dialectics, which, of course, ran counter to the dogmatic dialectical materialism of the GDR, even deliberately undermining it. In high school, he attended the branch of the school focused on natural sciences. As a result, he missed the opportunity to learn English at an early age, which he still regards as a major deficiency. Of course, history and German were taught, but they were oriented to interpretations that conformed with the system—even of classical German literature. For Gerber, the result was a conflict. He had to write school essays that could be interpreted as corresponding to the world view conveyed in school, while at the same time being compatible with the world view of his father. "This led to a dialectical way of thinking—not doing one thing while letting go of the other, but combining both with each other to form a whole. This later became one of the basic principles for my design: not giving up one idea in favor of another, but rather always finding a solution where one idea becomes possible without having to abandon the other." While mathematics, physics, and chemistry remained largely free of this ideological influence, students were intensively indoctrinated in biology and especially in history and German: "Our history lessons were essentially about revolutions and wars, starting with slave revolts and the like. The actual historical developments and social relations, on the other hand, were hardly taught to us, or not at all. Biology was shaped by the idea that human beings are formed exclusively by external influences; it thus focused on how human beings shaped other human beings. This was consistent with the interests of the system, since it rested on the assumption that all people could be educated to become Socialist Communists who followed the party line. The institution of the church and its followers, on the other hand, formed a center of opposition in the GDR early on, which for ideological reasons made them an unwelcome force.

Despite successfully completing high school, Gerber was not allowed to attend a university in the GDR for these same ideological reasons. His father then accepted a new parish post in Ruhlsdorf near Bernau, north of Berlin. Gerber's father wanted to give his children the opportunity to continue living with the family, but at the same time to travel to West Berlin to attend school or university. These last years, shortly before the construction of the Berlin Wall in August 1961, were marked by a certain schizophrenia in Berlin that is hardly imaginable today. On the one hand, it wasn't generally assumed that the GDR would once again completely close the

High school class of 1957, Geschwister-Scholl-Oberschule in Apolda, second from right, bottom row: Eckhard Gerber

city borders, as it had done during the blockade. And on the other hand, the status quo, with the two systems of East and West colliding directly in the city, was not sustainable in the long run. Moreover, the dramatically better supply situation and personal freedom in the West were much too enticing for those who were not committed GDR Socialists. Even though there were many checkpoints, it was still possible to move back and forth daily between East and West, between the political systems—for example, to live in the East and work in the West or to live in the East and go to school in the West.

Despite the move to Bernau, the Gerber family's situation in the GDR became increasingly difficult. As a Protestant pastor, the father was automatically regarded as an opponent of the Socialist regime. Eckhard Gerber himself belonged to the Junge Gemeinde and continued to refuse membership in the FDJ, or Freie Deutsche Jugend. In retrospect, it seems like an absurd late victory of the GDR school system that today—almost thirty years after the fall of the Berlin Wall—all of Berlin still offers a high school diploma after only twelve years of school and not thirteen, as is common elsewhere in Germany. While the decision to shorten high school by one year was regarded as a mistake and reversed in many West German federal states, in the capital state of Berlin people stubbornly insist on keeping the change. For Eckhard Gerber, his twelve-year school education in the GDR meant that his higher education entrance qualification was not recognized in the West. He therefore had to spend another year in school and take a second school exit exam in the West before being allowed to register at a West German university. For the twenty-year old, this meant an enormous change. Together with around thirty other young people, he spent a year studying at the Albert-Einstein-Oberschule (Albert Einstein High School) in Berlin-Britz, near Bruno Taut's horseshoe estate in what was then West Berlin. This was a class that had been set up especially for East Berlin high school graduates, as was found in almost all secondary schools in West Berlin. At that time, approximately 30 to 40 percent of East German high school graduates left the GDR, and the majority completed a West German high school diploma. In order to avoid a daily communte from his parents' apartment near Bernau via the Gesundbrunnen S-Bahn station, which was a border crossing to West Berlin, to Britz in the southeastern district of Neukölln, Gerber moved to a student residence on Martin-Luther-Straße, at the corner of Fuggerstraße, in Schöneberg, where other East German high school graduates were also staying. There, he lived in a room with six beds.

These were the years in which the German economic miracle also reached the three-sector city of West Berlin, at least to a moderate extent, and the western city center with its Zentrum am Zoo, including the Zoopalast and the famous Kaiser Wilhelm Memorial Church by Egon Eiermann, rose from the ruins of the war that still dominated the entire city. With the building exhibition Interbau 1957 in the Hansaviertel, the city pursued a new vision under its Senate Building Director Werner "Tüte" Düttmann, attempting to build on the international architectural developments of—Western—postwar modernism. This vision was deliberately intended to offer a contrast to the neoclassical *Zuckerbäckerstil,* or "wedding-cake style," of the "national tradition" realized on Stalinallee in East Berlin, in line with preferences at the time in the Eastern Bloc, before West Berlin, too, turned toward industrialized, prefabricated construction for both ideological and economic reasons. In addition to international architects such as Arne Jacobsen and Kay Fisker (Denmark), Alvar Aalto (Finland), Oscar Niemeyer (Brazil), Jacob Bakema (the Netherlands), and Pierro Vago (France), numerous German architects were also involved in this architectural experiment. Among them was Walter Gropius, the founder of the Bauhaus who was working at the time in exile in America, as well as Paul Baumgarten, a university professor in Berlin. The dispersed, open urban development, with individual high-rise towers in a green cityscape at the edge of the Tiergarten, formed an intentional alternative to the dense construction filling entire city blocks that was common from the *Gründerzeit.* Interbau left a deep impression on Gerber and on many of his later architectural colleagues. With it, a piece of modern city characterized by faith in the future and a will to innovate had emerged in war-torn Berlin. And in any case, everything in the West struck Gerber, the boy from Thuringia, as overwhelming—including the consumer goods on offer at the nearby KaDeWe, which he visited with his aunt, who lived in Dahlem, a former village at the edge of the city that had become a district of villas. Thirty years later, this experience of being a GDR citizen coming into contact with the West, as radical as it was confusing, would help Gerber better understand the East Germans who had to find their way almost overnight amid completely changed living conditions after reunification: "Later, after the fall of Communism, I repeatedly imagined myself in this position in order to understand the problems of citizens in the GDR, which became even more blatant after German reunification. Of course, I was still at the beginning of my training in West Berlin. My former school friends in the GDR had been working for a long time in 1990, and despite their fifty years or so of joyful anticipation of reunification, all of them suddenly lost their careers."

In the West, Gerber remained true to his passion, jazz. At the U-Bahn station Thielplatz in Dahlem, there was a jazz club, Eierschale (Eggshell), where he regularly went to hear concerts. He also managed to hear legends such as Sidney Bechet with his soprano saxophone, the trumpeter Dizzy Gillespie, or Benni Goodmann, who performed in the Deutschlandhalle. Gerber also frequently visited the Schillertheater in Berlin, where Johannna von Koczian regularly performed under the artistic director Boleslaw Barlog—she was an artist who especially impressed him. But the five West German marks that young people received every month from the Berlin Senate were hardly enough to let him live lavishly. Every now and then, a film at the Zoopalast or a visit to the café was all he could afford. Students at least were provided with tickets for public transit and with food.

Still, the adventure of West Berlin was not free of tension for Eckhard Gerber, the boy from East Germany. As a GDR citizen, he was frequently checked and searched by the East German police on his S-Bahn journeys from Bernau to West Berlin: "I once had a relatively large amount of money with me, about fifty ostmarks, and I was carrying it in coins, which led to inquiries. Finally, the police found my schoolbooks in my bag with the stamp of the Einstein High School in West Berlin. I was then interrogated at a police station in Pankow, and the pressure finally forced me to admit my intentions. I explained that after my *Abitur* in the GDR I had received an official rejection from the university, but that in the meantime I was taking trumpet lessons at an East Berlin conservatory (which was true). If I had not been admitted to study trumpet, my plan was to leave the GDR to study as a refugee in West Berlin or West Germany. In preparation, I was getting ready to take the Western high school examination at a West Berlin school."

It was not forbidden for GDR citizens to go to school or study in West Berlin. But it was certainly frowned upon. In addition, the GDR regime assumed that attending school or studying in West Berlin would require money, meaning it would be necessary to import currency from the GDR into the West in order to do so. And this was considered a serious crime. The fact that both school attendance and accommodation were provided free of charge by the Senate was unimaginable for the GDR police, and it was not possible to get them to grasp it. "My testimony was recorded as a statement that I was forced to sign, and then I was released. This incident scared me quite a bit, but surprisingly, it had no consequences for me."

For Gerber's father, the situation at his new parish post in Ruhlsdorf near Bernau became even worse. His Sunday sermons, in which he preached a Christian message that inherently failed to "conform with the system," as Eckhard Gerber remembers, resulted in his father's being reported by an informer for "inciting a boycott." "The public prosecutor's office had a warrant for his arrest, but a friend tipped him off with enough time for the family to flee the GDR in a hurry, via the Gesundbrunnen S-Bahn station." The wall had not yet been built, but the borders were already being controlled, which meant it was no longer possible to simply cross over to West Berlin. The only way to flee was thus via the S-Bahn to Friedrichstraße, which crossed through a small tip of West Berlin at Gesundbrunnen, where it was possible to get off the train. The large family traveled in separate groups so as not to attract attention; but this also meant they couldn't bring along larger suitcases. Like his friend Dietrich Sattler's family before him, Eckhard Gerber had to leave the places of his childhood behind for good—or at least for the foreseeable future—with only a few belongings in his luggage. For him, his farewell from the GDR in 1958 took place in installments, as it were: after the first step of his schooling in West Berlin, a completely new, liberated chapter was to begin with his secondary school years and then his studies at the university in Braunschweig. For Gerber's father, however, the old chapter did not end with his flight from the GDR. As a Protestant pastor he came under massive criticism from the east-west German church leadership because he had left the GDR. The leadership was riven by open dissent. Bishop Otto Dibelius, who officially presided over all of Berlin, and his ministerial commissioner Kurt Scharf, who would later succeed Dibelius in office, decreed that Gerber had to return to the East. But Gerber refused, referring to his duty to care for his six children. A church disciplinary procedure was then initiated against Gerber, which lasted two years and ended with a negative outcome for the pastor. It was only later, before a proper German court, that Hans Gerber finally received justice. He was not compelled to return to the GDR and was allowed to continue his profession as a pastor in the Federal Republic of Germany. During these legal proceedings and the uncertainty they caused, the family lived from social welfare and the help of friends in Wachenheim, a small village along the German Wine Road in Rhineland-Palatinate, until Hans Gerber, by then fifty-two years old, was given a new parish post in Schleswig-Holstein, in Bosau on the Großer Plöner See (Great Plöner Lake). Despite the economic restrictions after the family escaped from the GDR, Gerber remembers the summer spent along the Wine Road as a wonderful

The class of students from East Germany studying at the West Berlin high school on a class trip to Schleswig-Holstein, 1957•1958

After completing high school in West Berlin, departure to West Germany from Tempelhof Airport, 1958

time. During the semester break, it was a place where the family was finally reunited, and they were free of the spying and the restrictions they had experienced in the GDR. "We enjoyed the wine region and above all the incredible freedom to finally be able to say what one thinks, to finally do creative things oneself without any restrictions from anyone or any institution." In the meantime, Gerber's eldest brother Eberhard had begun studying medicine in Marburg, Gotthard was continuing his studies of church music in Frankfurt with Helmut Walcha, Volkhard had become a lawyer and would later live near his parents in Lübeck, Manhard had completed a business degree in Hamburg, and Gerber's sister Mechthild was still going to school. And Eckhard Gerber? Despite his experience constructing an apiary and stables, the profession of architect was not something that he initially had in mind. For even though building and drawing had always interested and fascinated him, "the architectural profession did not tempt me given the overall situation in the GDR. Everything to do with construction was politically fraught and ideologically controlled." In West Germany, with a West German high school diploma, no one could prevent him from studying for political reasons. He first considered becoming a pediatrician. The decision to study architecture was ultimately made in a conversation with his mother. "'Eckhard, why don't you study architecture, you're so good at craftsmanship?' She certainly had no real idea at all of what such a profession requires and entails, but somehow parents have an instinct for their children's basic talents. I can see that today with my own children. This career choice also really appealed to my father, and so I withdrew my matriculation for medical studies at the Universität Hamburg and took things as they came."

Gerber earned his first paycheck after graduating from high school in the West from a construction company in Mannheim that carried out projects at BASF: "I showed up at the office to introduce myself based on an ad. I got a critical look and a comment: 'But you know that this is real physical work?' I said yes and started one morning at 7 a.m. The pay was 1.53 D-marks an hour, which was a lot of money for me back then." Rapid learning effects were included: "We all stood there in the morning, in a row, and the foreman assigned us to work. I got a foreman who explained to me what I had to do. I was used to completing my job as quickly as possible in order to be done with the work. And that's what I did here, too, at the construction site. So I finished my job, thinking: 'Great!' And then I sat down on a rock. The foreman came up to me and berated me, wondering what I was thinking.

I'd hardly started working and I was already loafing around. I told him I'd finished the work assigned to me. 'Then you'll have to do something else,' he said. Afterwards, a coworker who had observed all of this took me aside and explained that on the construction site you always have to show that you are busy. Even when you've done your job, you just have to look around and take a beam, lay it over your shoulder and carry it from one side of the construction site to the other. That would be enough, 'then you won't stand out.'" But there were also situations that Gerber could have done without. A few days later, he was supposed to balance unsecured over a free beam at a height of about ten meters in order to lay down more beams together with his colleagues. "I refused to do this work because I was far too afraid to fall down from up there. After a sharp exchange of words with the foreman, I told him that my hourly wage of 1.53 marks was far too low to carry out such a dangerous job. He looked at me, I think somewhat in agreement, and he let it go." Exhausted from the difficult work, but happy, Gerber came home in the evening. The work gave him valuable lessons for his own construction later on. It taught him "deep respect and esteem for the workers at the construction site."

In order to get an impression of the new parish office in Bosau and the situation in the church, but above all to make sure the parish office would approve his appointment, Hans Gerber sent his youngest son Manhard together with Eckhard to the hilly area of Holstein called Holstein Switzerland. The parsonage still had to be rebuilt and renovated, so the two boys stayed with the sexton, who gave them a loving welcome. After their involuntary detours through the history and landscape of Germany, Bosau was soon to become the Gerber family's home—even though after 1959, the family's first sunny summer in Bosau, with lots of swimming in the Großer Plöner See, most of the children only came home during their semester breaks. When they did, they all lived in the parsonage with the thatched roof, right beside the Romanesque church—a so-called Vicelinus church from the twelfth century—that sat directly on the lake. In Bosau, too, Gerber immediately looked for work. He found employment at a masonry construction company and carpentry shop, slowly but surely sliding deeper and deeper into the construction business while also earning some money. "First, I had to do some work on the gang saw, a cutting machine that cut logs into beams and the beams into boards and planks.

It was beautiful to see how the round tree trunk was cut into individual, long wooden discs. But before the machine could get to work, the tree bark

Church in Bosau at the
Großer Plöner See

Parsonage in Bosau

had to be removed from the trunks, which was a laborious job that took place outside the workshop." With the onset of winter, Gerber again lost his seasonal job in Bosau and subsequently went looking for another job in the nearby town of Eutin. For this company, his task was to help design a new area to be developed directly at Plöner See. "This work was completely new to me, but I did my best and in the end was able to complete the plan by carrying out discussions with the relevant experts." In the spring, he returned to work for the Bosau construction company, where he was now assigned to build wells. At the time, there was no central water supply for the village. Again, he learned lessons that would last him a lifetime: "I learned that there were basically two different types of wells: filter wells and dug wells. There were only three or four of us assigned to this task. The foreman, Fritz Dombrowski, had the ability to find the underground water-bearing veins with a divining rod. Until then I thought it was hocus-pocus, but finding water with a divining rod is actually a special ability. At first, I didn't believe him. So he gave me the divining rod, which I braced firmly in my hands. But nothing happened when I held it. Then he stood behind me, with my arms in his two hands, and walked with me across the property. And indeed, the divining rod then pulled toward the ground, and I was unable to hold it back. That convinced me and also gave me confidence in the foreman. He was an alcoholic and always had to drink his schnapps on the side. Maybe the alcohol was necessary, too, for his divining-rod powers to function." Dombrowski had the gift of being able to determine exactly where, in what quantities, and at what depth the water was to be found. His findings were the basis for our decision as to whether to construct a filter well or a dug well. Usually, dug wells were necessary. "A tripod was placed over the spot where the well was to be dug. It consisted of three beams that were connected to each other at the top and placed three-legged, so to speak, over the hole. In the middle, there was a wheel at the top, over which a rope was led, from which a bucket was hung. We then lowered this bucket into the hole we were digging, which was about one meter in diameter. After about forty centimeters, a concrete ring was laid and the earth was further excavated inside the concrete ring so that the ring could slide further down into the earth. Then additional concrete rings with a diameter of one meter and a height of fifty centimeters were laid on top of each other, one at a time, and we kept digging until the well reached a depth of between eight and twelve meters." Gerber had to dig out the earth and deposit it into the bucket, which was then pulled up. The deeper one got, the muddier the work became. "And it was very dangerous, though I didn't realize that until much later. You worked without a helmet and without any protective clothing. Thank God, nothing happened."

In their free time, Eckhard Gerber and his siblings became acquainted with the Bosau village school teacher and his wife, who had two good-looking daughters. This was reason enough for the Gerber boys to occasionally stop by the family's yard. During a game of skat, Gerber also met a friend of the family, Mr. Pauly. He had a holiday home on Plöner See. Pauly worked in Hamburg for an American advertising agency and was married to the actress Lotte Rausch. Her role as Mother Schölermann in the eponymous TV series made her one of the first German TV icons. Impressed by Gerber and his dedication at the building site, Pauly suggested that he introduce himself to the Reemtsma company in Hamburg, which had just launched a scholarship program for talented young people. Together they drove to Hamburg to the Reemtsma Park and villa, where they made an appointment with the executive board responsible for the foundation to support outstanding students that had been established by the brothers Hermann F. and Philipp F. Reemtsma. Gerber, who had just registered to study at the university in Braunschweig, was asked about his architectural studies and why he had chosen the subject, where he came from, and where he wanted to go.

Did he know, for instance, that the new buildings for the Reemtsma administration had been realized in 1952 by Godber Nissen, who was also responsible for renovating the Reemtsma villa designed by Martin Elsässer in the Weimar Republic? All the same, the foundation's decision to accept him into its scholarship program gave him a certain economic independence in the following years and allowed him to concentrate on his studies. And he didn't experience the requirement that he present regular reports on his progress to the program in Hamburg as a constraint.

In order to escape the conscription introduced in the Federal Republic of Germany in 1956, Gerber had to begin his studies in the summer semester of 1959. However, the regular start of his studies would not have been until the winter semester of 1959/60. After initially receiving no reply to his application, he traveled from Bosau to Braunschweig, where he went to the Dean's Office: "A Mr. Meine received me and informed me that it would only be possible to begin studies in the winter semester, but that everything would be difficult anyway due to changes in the admission procedure."

That answer didn't satisfy Gerber at all. He worked to get an appointment with Konrad Hecht, who was responsible for the admission of first-year

Technische Universität Braunschweig with high-rise by Dieter Oesterlen

students. At first, in vain. But Gerber remained persistent until he was successful: "Professor Hecht welcomed me with a critical look and explained to me that he could not just automatically accept me into the program, since an entrance examination was required beginning in the winter semester. He nevertheless spoke with me to determine whether I was suited to study architecture. Much of what he asked concerning architectural and art history was unfamiliar to me with my GDR background. Of course, he also wanted to know why I badly wanted to start studying in the summer semester, which I also explained. Finally, he asked me to make a sketch of his office, where I had waited for our interview. I was lucky that I still had a very clear memory of the room and was able to sketch it well in a floor plan with furnishings and a cross section. Hecht looked briefly at the sketch, looked at me and said: 'You are accepted.'"

The Braunschweig School

For German postwar architecture, the Braunschweig school was an institution. Its influential antipode was the Karlsruhe school in the south of Germany, which was shaped by Egon Eiermann's work and teaching. What both universities had in common was their clear focus on a consistent modernist architecture, which their leading figures realized in their own works and also imparted to their students. The differing architectural approaches of the teachers produced a certain range in how the formal language of modernism was elaborated. In Braunschweig, Dieter Oesterlen, Friedrich Wilhelm Kraemer, and Walter Henn (who had come to Braunschweig from Dresden) determined the curriculum. All three pursued clearly different philosophies when it came to teaching, as Gerber remembers: "Kraemer was the intellectual teacher who conveyed an ethical stance to us in his Friday evening lectures, which he always held in front of a crowded auditorium. But he also gave us an understanding of clear, functional basic structures in simple buildings, which he explained, for example, using three matchboxes: lying flat, standing flat, and standing on edge. Dieter Oesterlen taught us how to develop successful designs that could win architectural competitions, and also how to think like an architect, as well as the craft of construction. Henn was the rigorous functionalist and engineering design teacher. For me as a student, all three professors complemented each other superbly." Kraemer, who was very successful in Germany at the time, also introduced the students to the contemporary building development and architecture from the United States that had been so influential for his own work. Since the beginning of the 1950s, a completely new generation of skyscrapers emerged there, so-called skin and bones buildings consisting of a supporting frame of steel and a glass curtain wall. In addition to Gordon Bunshaft's work for Skidmore, Owings & Merrill, for which Bunshaft realized the legendary Lever House in New York in 1951/52, the architecture of those years was shaped by the work of Ludwig Mies van der Rohe, the former director of the Bauhaus who had immigrated to the United States. Mies set new standards with his iconic Seagram Building in New York, the campus of the Illinois Institute of Technology, and the apartment buildings he designed in Chicago. At the same time, he combined the prewar modernist architecture of the Weimar Republic with the international influences of the postwar period. Kraemer's direct engagement with Mies's masterful work was concretely reflected in his own projects—at the Dortmund Aufbau- und Abendgymnasium (1956–1959), for example, or the City Tower in Essen (1961–1963).

Dieter Oesterlen, 1991 (*left*) and Friedrich Wilhelm Kraemer, 1965 (*right*), teachers of Eckhard Gerber at the Technische Universität Braunschweig

And while Oesterlen's architectural signature was no less modern than that of the Kraemers, it nevertheless appeared less austere and cooly functionalistic, even with its elegance. This may reflect Oesterlen's somewhat different training. Oesterlen was shaped by Paul Schmitthenner and the conservative Stuttgart school Schmitthenner founded, and before the war Oesterlen studied with Heinrich Tessenow and Hans Poelzig in Berlin. These two architects denote distinct poles of modernity: Tessenow's buildings were more classical in their clear and calm formal language, such as with the Festspielhaus in Dresden-Hellerau; Hans Poelzig's works, by contrast, were clearly more expressive and characterized by a strong, colorful style, such as his Haus des Rundfunks or the Friedrichstadtpalast, both in Berlin. Despite all their differences, however, both Tessenow and Poelzig integrated traditional qualities of architectural craftsmanship into their buildings, and despite the modernity of their buildings, neither allowed their work to be reduced to the typical square shapes of the modern Bauhaus aesthetic. Oesterlen's works oscillated between these poles. They had nothing in common with the expressive, brutal concrete power of Marcel Breuer, whose buildings and furniture were antagonists, as it were, to the cool cubic forms that Mies built in American exile. At the same time, Oesterlen's architecture was marked by a subtlety of its own that is equally evident in his Braunschweiger Universitätshochhaus (1954–1956), his Historisches Museum in Hanover (1964–1967), or his church designs. In Braunschweig, he offered a series of lectures—"Das Detail im Gesamtentwurf," or "The detail in the overall design"—that made a lasting impression on Gerber. "He showed us his projects from the beginning of the design for the competition to their implementation. I especially remember the project for the new state parliament in Lower-Saxony, which was being built on the ruins of the old Leine Palace, where the Hanoverian kings had reigned. Oesterlen transformed the building into an outstanding symbiosis of the old and the new. But he also showed us his design for a church in Sennestadt near Bielefeld, the design with which he had just won a competition. He asked us to keep our fingers crossed for him so that he would get the commission, which was in fact what happened. The church turned out very beautifully. He had also built a church and parish center for the Zwölf Apostel (twelve apostle) congregation in Hildesheim—a complex consisting of a church, a parish hall, a parsonage, and a kindergarten for which he had also won a competition. The overall concept was shaped according to the design principle of free folding, producing a highly sculptural effect. Oesterlen's lecture on his competition design for the former concentration

Parliament of Lower Saxony in Hanover, revitalization of the old castle by Dieter Oesterlen, 1954•1962

Zwölf-Apostel-Kirche, community center in Hildesheim by Dieter Oesterlen, 1964•1967, competition model

Versöhnungskirche, Dachau, Helmut Striffler, 1965•1967

camp in Dachau was especially significant. It was characteristic for him that he presented the designs of the other prizewinners in addition to his own contribution." This allowed the students to learn what it took to participate in a competition and also to win it. At the same time, Oesterlen taught the students to have respect for the best design, even if it was not one's own, as in the case of the Versöhnungskirche, or Church of Reconciliation, in the former Nazi concentration camp in Dachau. The commission was awarded to Helmut Striffler from Mannheim, who had received his training in Karlsruhe. Oesterlen presented both his own design and Striffler's to the students. "He had clearly explained to us why Striffler's design offered the best concept by far, which he acknowledged ungrudgingly. I still consider the Versöhnungskirche in the Dachau concentration camp to be one of the best postwar buildings in Germany." Realized from 1965 to 1967, Striffler's Versöhnungskirche is a building of sheer concrete impressiveness, slightly sunken into the ground, sparse in its formal language, and yet also powerful and touching. A masterpiece of German postwar modernism.

Although Gerber learned a lot from Oesterlen, he ultimately decided on Kraemer as an advisor for his thesis. Kraemer was not only the better known of the two Braunschweig professors but also the more intellectual architect, in contrast to Oesterlen, who was more strongly influenced by a focus on construction. These qualities held an equally strong appeal to Gerber as Kraemer's approach to design. Kraemer "produced very structured and clear projects," Gerber remembers. The first generation of teachers at the Braunschweig school also included Konrad Hecht, a building researcher and building historian whom Gerber had met immediately upon registering. Hecht, too, would continue to play an important role for Gerber. Because of his education in the GDR, and despite having completed the Western high school examination, Gerber felt he had shortcomings in history and cultural matters for which one year of school in the West had not allowed him to compensate. That was why he made all the more effort to learn the basics of architectural history that Hecht taught. "I absolutely wanted to acquire this missing knowledge and understand the historical and cultural contexts that form the basis for architecture and so much more. In preparing a presentation for Hecht's course on "Building during the Baroque Period," Gerber conducted library research in the Herzog August Bibliothek in Wolfenbüttel that had been recently renovated by Friedrich Wilhelm Kraemer. This prompted him to ask about the kind of architecture that lay dormant beneath the lavish furnishings and paintings that characterize Baroque buildings.

What he ultimately found was a very simple, clearly structured, and geometric art of construction. The building's specific character emerged first though the baroque decoration. Hence whereas Gerber was catching up in cultural history, he found it easier to study subjects based on natural scientific principles, such as structural design and statics, building materials science, concrete construction, and descriptive geometry. In retrospect, one thing he criticizes about his studies is that "up to the preliminary examination, design was not taught at all," and that there were no design exercises. The students first of all had to amass and grasp crucial architectural knowledge about supporting frameworks, reinforced concrete, and building construction, as well as descriptive geometry, building technology, building materials science, and the like. The same was true for artistic subjects, such as the basics of design, freehand drawing, and so on.

In contrast to Oesterlen and Kraemer, the Croatian-born Zdenko Strižić (who like Oesterlen had studied architecture with Hans Poelzig) was among the professors in Braunschweig whom Gerber perceived more through their theoretical influence than through their buildings. Yet Strižić, too, realized many projects. For example, he designed the Institute for Steel Construction at the TU Braunschweig, completed in 1972. Strižić is said to have especially appreciated the open and free working atmosphere in Poelzig's studio, where he collaborated in designing the cinema Babylon in Berlin. Strižić was not only known for his interior and furniture designs but was also regarded as an excellent photographer.

Gerber vividly recalls a student excursion in 1962 with Strižić during which they viewed, among other things, Le Corbusier's work in southern France, including the Unité d'Habitation in Marseilles, the chapel in Ronchamp, and the monastery of La Tourette, an icon of exposed concrete Brutalism that had just been completed in 1960. Gerber would later take his own students on similar excursions into modernity. "Particularly interesting for us as students was a discussion between Kraemer and Strižić in which Strižić wanted to convey the idea to us that office or hotel buildings, for instance, have no corridors. Kraemer objected, arguing that it was obvious one could not do without corridors for the allocation of rooms in the floor plan. But Strižić insisted on his position: 'There are no corridors.' I've remembered that to this day. When we are working on designs in which corridors are of course necessary, we always question whether it might not be better to transform a long, shapeless corridor into a beautiful, open, elongated space."

Administrative building of the Unterharzer Hüttenwerke in Goslar, Friedrich Wilhelm Kraemer, 1959

In 1962, Gerber passed his intermediate examination. This was the starting signal for "the more beautiful period of study connected to design." He benefited from the experience he had already gained in his practical work at the construction site and in various architectural offices. However, his training in design at the university continued to progress only slowly. It took one semester or even more to develop designs. And the students were not taught much about the design process itself. "It would have been important for me to learn more about the criteria that should be used to formulate a draft. What kind of design tools were available at all? How does one proceed in the individual steps of the design process? During my studies, these remained open questions for me."

These deficits in training prompted Gerber to formulate a clearly structured curriculum for his own teaching at the universities in Wuppertal and Essen. He provided his students with a set of tools they could use to independently work out solutions for the respective construction tasks.

It was clear to Gerber from an early age that, after studying architecture, he wanted to work in his own office as an independent architect. That was one reason that already as a student he became intensively involved with the journal *Architektur und Wettbewerbe* (Architecture and competitions), published by the leading German architectural publisher of the time, the Karl Krämer Verlag in Stuttgart—the same publishing house in which Reyner Banham's epoch-making book *Brutalismus in der Architektur* (Brutalism in architecture) appeared. Why was the magazine such important reading for him? "For each competition, the magazine presented the scope of the project and its requirements followed by the prize jury's assessment of the submissions. In addition, the designs were shown with floor plans, cross sections, elevations, and a site plan, including a model. I studied these competitions very intensively to understand why one work was better than the other. By intensively studying and understanding the assessments of the prize juries, I was able to grasp bit by bit what was right or wrong, better or not so good, and where the core ideas of a design lay. I could then apply this thinking to my own work." Full of curiosity, Gerber sought out reference points for his work, also coming across the buildings of Günter Behnisch, who belonged to the group of especially successful German architects in the mid-1960s who broke new ground in architecture and won many competitions. Behnisch's conception of architecture is still exemplified today by the congenial Olympic Park he built in Munich for the 1972 Olympic Games, with its open structure and borrowings from high-tech modernism, which he developed with his partners for a competition and then realized with the structural engineer Frei Otto. Gerber intensively studied the work of Behnisch, whom he understood as a counterpole to Roland Ostertag: "In contrast to Behnisch's open structures, Ostertag built what looked like castles. For me, it was interesting to see which of these two different approaches to architecture had a viable future. And that was clearly Behnisch! Ostertag's concepts, which tended to be final, were not open enough; his buildings did not allow for further development." But it was not only Behnisch's avant-garde architectural attitude, ready for the future, that interested Gerber, but also Behnisch's intuition as an entrepreneur. Gerber's first personal contact with Behnisch took place in Darmstadt, at the university where Behnisch was teaching and where Gerber had applied for a position on the faculty. When it became apparent that Gerber would not get this job, Behnisch let Gerber know right away, long before the official notification of his rejection, encouraging him instead to quickly apply elsewhere. They later met again as colleagues on prize juries, for example, on a project in Nuremberg. "I had actually assumed that Behnisch would chair the jury, as an older and more renowned architect. But he didn't want to, arguing that I should do it instead. In fact, the jury meeting turned out to be quite interesting for me because it showed me how things can develop in discussions in a completely different way than expected. There was one contribution that I found to be very good, but which was excluded in the second round because it offered only 70 percent of the required usable area. Competitions always have two different components: On the one hand, designs that can be built are sought out and recognized with prizes. That's what the prize categories are for. And on the other hand, the competition serves to further later architectural discussions, for example, in trade journals. In addition to the works that win awards, this also includes designs designated as special mentions that cannot be built because of the project's requirements, but which sometimes contain ideas that are particularly worthy of discussion. These projects are not lower-quality designs but contain extraordinary ideas less suitable for the realization of the project, which we as experts would like to see discussed. That's why, in Nuremberg, I reintroduced the submission that had already been eliminated, arguing that it shouldn't be built. 'Let's designate this design as a special mention in order to keep it in the running.' Behnisch offered me strong support for this idea. In the end, it turned out that none of the designs were really suitable for realization. We thus awarded two second prizes, with the proviso that they be revised by the architects. One of the two was the submission that had initially been eliminated because the usable area it offered was too small. After revision, this design was in fact the best work by far. It now included all of the required usable area, with the same concept. The design received the first prize and was ultimately realized. Today, the project is even depicted on the brown highway signs in the area around Nuremberg."

When Gerber last met Günter Behnisch in Stuttgart, Behnisch told him something that is still centrally important for young architectural firms today: "In every one of your projects, you must find one member of the client committee who is committed to your design, who takes on this project as his or her own. Otherwise, you may fail."

Alongside the high points of architecture from which Gerber sought orientation at the end of his studies in Braunschweig as he developed his own path, attitude, and style, everyday life also made its demands—which the prospective architect, as one of six children, had to meet on his own through hard work. The Reemtsma Foundation scholarship gave him a good basic level of security. This was supplemented by regular work—at first on the construction site and later in an architectural firm. He found a third economic foundation in his passion for jazz.

After his third semester, Gerber found a job during the semester break in Hanns Rietschel's architectural office in Eutin, a town about fifteen kilometers from Bosau. For him, this job was an important encounter with the day-to-day business of an architect. "I got to know planning work from the preliminary draft to the design, construction documentation, and tender; at times, I came along to the construction site and quickly grasped how a planning process worked through to the realization of a building, including filing documentation, folding up the plans, creating blueprints, putting together a building application, and the like. With the small projects, which were mostly conversions or detached houses, everything was manageable, so that I quickly learned the craft of planning."

Gerber, the student, quickly contributed his own fresh ideas to the small office's competition department, designing a high school in Lütjenburg, a church center, kindergartens, and a savings bank in Burg auf Fehmarn. With the high school in Lütjenburg, he successfully achieved an honorable mention.

And then there was the music. Gerber's passion for jazz led him to Kiel, where Louis Armstrong gave a concert in the Ostseehalle in February 1959. While roaming the city waiting for the concert, Gerber ran into the legendary jazz trumpeter, who had just left his hotel. Gerber boldly stood in Armstrong's way and asked for his autograph. Armstrong pushed Gerber aside and made it clear he was in a hurry to get to the rehearsal for his concert. Together with his older fellow student Wolfgang Wigger, who played guitar and banjo, Gerber founded the Lion-Town-Jazzband in Braunschweig. During the semester they performed on weekends in a former bunker, the well-known Studio 2 on Wilhelmstraße in the same city. On the ground floor, bands played Dixieland, blues and modern jazz, while on the upper floor, dance music came from a jukebox and the girls wore petticoats—two completely contrary worlds. The gigs in the jazz bunker meant a nice bit of extra income: five marks an hour, which for six hours of jazz meant thirty marks on a Saturday. This almost financed the monthly rent for Gerber's room at Walter-Flex-Straße 17 on the east side of Braunschweig, which is where Gerber lived, about half an hour on foot from the university, until the end of his studies in 1965. "My landlady, Mrs. Sperling, didn't really want to have a student as a tenant but rather a 'decent worker' who would travel home on the weekends. But she must have liked me after all. During the semester, the room cost forty marks a month, and during the holidays, it was thirty-five."

Together with the salary Gerber earned in Rietschel's architectural office, he was able to afford his first car in 1961, a Maico Champion, for three hundred and fifty marks. After a piston seized, he replaced the car with a brand-new white Fiat 500, a legendary small car with a sunroof. At the time, it cost five thousand marks. At the beginning of the sixties, jazz was already starting to fall out of favor. Fewer and fewer visitors came to Studio 2 for the jazz evenings, which faced competition from beat music and rock and roll. In 1960, the Liverpool band the Beatles had their first performances in the Star-Club in Hamburg, and two years later they had an international breakthrough with "Love Me Do." For Gerber's band, this meant they had to change their musical direction. They would drive by car nearly fifty kilometers to Goslar, to the rustic restaurant Gosetal, in the forest of the Harz mountains, to play dance music on Saturday evenings and Sunday afternoons. And during the semester break, Gerber played in another band in Eutin.

While Gerber's studies in Braunschweig slowly came to an end, he continued to gain practical experience in architecture firms. He also took part in a student competition organized by the brick industry. He intensively took up the task of designing a farm with dairy cows. He familiarized himself with the latest methods of animal farming, with how the animals were fed

SIEGER EINES WETTBEWERBS zwischen mehreren Jazzkapellen während eines von der Schülermitverwaltung Braunschweiger Gymnasien im Schützenhaus veranstalteten Oktoberballs wurde die „lion-town-jazzband" (unser Bild). Ein Phonmesser registrierte den Applaus für die drei Kapellen. Mit der Aufführung des Einakters „Der Mörder" von Curt Goetz hatte die Veranstaltung begonnen. Ehrengäste waren Frau Oberbürgermeister Fuchs und Stadtjugendpfleger Willi Staake.

Foto: Steffens

Konzert am 27.10. / in der Braunschweiger Zeitung / am 29.10.1960 /

The Lion Town jazz band in Braunschweig, (*from left*) Eckhard Gerber (trumpet), Uwe Schollmeyer (trombone), Wilhelm Remmer (clarinet), Claus-Dieter Bäth (percussion), 1960, *Braunschweiger Zeitung*

The Lion Town jazz band on tour, (*from left*) Claus-Dieter Bäth (percussion), Wolfgang Wigger (banjo), Joachim Sordel (double bass), Wilhelm Remmer (clarinet), Eckhard Gerber (trumpet), Uwe Schollmeyer (trombone), 1960•1961

Wilhelm Remmer and Fritz Masendorf
in front of Eckhard Gerber's car,
a Messerschmitt Champion, 1961

Eckhard Gerber with his new
Fiat 500, 1963

and the manure removed from the stalls. "My design was based on a silage silo plant (Harvestore). I developed a very simple, functional concept and designed the buildings with a prefabricated brick panel system. The design won first prize, which of course made me very happy."

This student work already revealed characteristic aspects of Gerber's future architecture: a precise analysis of the task and a comprehensive collecting of available knowledge in order to develop a functional and clear design. But what does the path of a successful architect look like? What defines success as an architect? In order to gain further practical experience and earn the money he needed, at the end of his studies Gerber applied with Hans-Peter Diedrichsen and Rüdiger Hoge in Kiel for a holiday job, which was considered at the time to be one of the leading architectural firms in Schleswig-Holstein. "Hoge had been Friedrich Wilhelm Kraemer's assistant and was involved in outstanding projects realized in the spirit of the Braunschweig school. I contacted him and was invited to a conversation. His question to me was whether I wanted to work in a good office or earn money. I said, of course, that I wanted to do both, work in a good office and earn money. He told me that I could work for him in a good office, but I couldn't earn any money."

It's hard to imagine that a young architect would have received such an answer in an Anglo-Saxon architectural firm. In the German cultural sector, on the other hand, this has unfortunately been typical for a long time. Economic success in this country was almost inevitably accompanied by doubts about the artistic quality of the works produced. This corresponds to the completely absurd distinction between "serious art" and "entertainment," an overly exaggerated opposition that is also quite foreign to Anglo-Saxon cultures. The consequences of this cultural snobbishness have been regrettable for German architects. For example, the lack of appreciation for the economic success of architectural firms in their own country has contributed to the fact that German architects, in contrast to their international colleagues, still play a rather subordinate role worldwide. In addition, ubiquitous envy ensures that the few internationally renowned German architects hardly receive the esteem and appreciation they deserve within Germany—which is quite different than the situation in Denmark or Great Britain, to give two examples.

After this sobering answer, Gerber's path led for three months to Schnittger Architects, whose office was also in Kiel, instead of to Diedrichsen and Hoge. Shaped by the fresh ideas he was able to acquire during his studies, he was

IN DER WANDELHALLE der Technischen Hochschule sind die preisgekrönten Modelle des Ideenwettbewerbs der Ziegelindustrie Niedersachsens ausgestellt. Unser Bild: Kommilitonen der Gewinner Eckhard Gerber und Friedrich-Karl Winkler „studieren" die Entwürfe der Sieger. Foto: Steffens

Ideenwettbewerb der Ziegelindustrie:

„Ein sehr gutes Resultat"

13 Entwürfe für landwirtschaftliche Betriebe preisgekrönt

Willkommene Studienbeihilfen für 13 Studenten der Fachrichtung Bauwesen an der Technischen Hochschule: Mit ansehnlichen Barschecks honorierten die Fachverbände der Ziegel- und Dachziegelindustrie Niedersachsens die Ideen der Preisträger eines Studentenwettbewerbs, den sie schaftlichen Bauwesen für das Mauerwerk und das Dach" im Herbst 1963 ausgeschrieben hatten.

22 Kandidaten der Architektur entwarfen und planten einen „streng rationalisierten und gut funktionierenden landwirtschaftlichen Betrieb, der nur vom Bauern selbst und einem

Fellow students examining models from the first competition won by Eckhard Gerber, 1964

Diploma thesis by Eckhard Gerber,
parish center with church, parish
hall, parsonage, kindergarten,
and nursing home, 1966

immediately hired there at a good salary in the competition and design department. But Gerber's employment at Schnittger also turned out to be a short episode: "The architectural quality and atmosphere didn't appeal to me. I knew that, if I had my own office, I wouldn't work like this! That was the main thing I learned there." Together with his fellow student Manfred Lange, with whom Gerber had worked in the art room in Braunschweig, Gerber took part in competitions toward the end of his studies. "Having a spot in a art room was enormously important to us. We came here in the morning, just as if it were a job, and then headed home in the evening, often quite late. We worked all day and learned from discussions with the other students, many of whom were further along in their studies or not as far along as we were. In this way, even at the university we learned and practiced the practicalities of the work that ultimately happens in an office.

Following the competition he had already won for the nursing home in Eutin, Gerber, working together with Lange, now won a competition for a secondary school in Hallenberg near Winterberg, which they crafted as a so-called submarine, i.e., on behalf of an architect who was already practicing, in this case the office of Rüsten in Meschede. This was a success of lasting importance, because it proved to be an important step for Gerber. Unlike many of his fellow students in Braunschweig, this successful competition did not lead Gerber to head to the north of the Federal Republic, where his parents also lived, but to the west. Gerber intensively supported his fellow student Lange in completing his diploma thesis. Gerber himself did not complete his studies until the autumn of 1966. In June 1966, Gerber and Lange had rented an office in Meschede and, in cooperation with von Rüsten, had already taken on the commission for the secondary school. It was to be the first joint project of the office that Lange and Gerber would share in the future in Meschede. It was June 1966 before Gerber passed his last exams. Afterwards, all students had to present their work in an exhibition, allowing the professors to see whether the respective candidates had the necessary maturity to work on their diploma thesis. It was a very first work exhibition for the students, combining exercises and designs. "I still remember Friedrich Wilhelm Kraemer's visit to my exhibition stand. He took an interested and careful look at my work, since there were competition designs hanging there in addition to my student projects. This was something he particularly liked, and he praised the results."

Together with Manfred Lange, Gerber then worked on the early sketches, final design, and building application for the school in Hallenberg. "This work happened relatively quickly for the time, and in a short period we received a fee that was quite high for us at the time. This put us in a position to immediately work on further competitions." In Meschede, already working in his own office space, Gerber devoted himself to his diploma thesis. But before that, he successfully submitted designs in two more competitions. "The topic of my thesis, which was directed by Kraemer, was a community center with a church, parish hall, kindergarten, and a nursing home. This was a relatively large construction task, which also made high demands in terms of urban development because it was a very difficult piece of land to work with. I remember well how I transported my diploma thesis to Braunschweig by car, together with the large model of the church with its tower."

In November 1966, at the presentation of diploma certificates, Gerber gave a speech on behalf of the students that was also attended by the professors. To Gerber, it seemed like a journey through time when an exhibition of works by former Braunschweig students was shown in 2015. It included his own diploma thesis. Gerber gave a short lecture about his studies and the Braunschweig school of the sixties in the same overcrowded auditorium where Friedrich Wilhelm Kraemer's Friday evening lectures had taken place.

Meanwhile, in Meschede

The Königsmünster Abbey towers high above the small town of Meschede in the Sauerland. Its mighty, brick-red double tower façade is visible from afar. Inside, the Benedictine abbey (designed by the Cologne architect Hans Schilling) houses a marvelous sacred space. It is impressive not only in its size, but also because of its atmosphere. The atmosphere immediately surrounds visitors and prompts them to fall silent amid the colored twilight that is spilling through room's few windows. The Protestant parson's son and newly graduated architect also fell under the spell of the interior of this Catholic church, which had only been recently consecrated. Fifty years later, on a cool February morning, we visit the abbey together, standing silently in front of the altar screen on which colorful reflections of light dance. Here, in the Abbey of Königsmünster, space and faith, time and art, are condensed together to create a special unity showing what architecture can achieve, if only you open yourself up to it. For this day, we have planned to visit three buildings in Meschede built between 1966 and 1976 that are exemplary for the years Gerber spent in the town: The Volksbank in the city center, the hillside terrace houses, and one of the detached houses designed by the young Eckhard Gerber.

Two years after the Königsmünster Abbey was consecrated as a "peace church in a world that cannot find peace," the two recently graduated architects Gerber and Lange founded their Werkgemeinschaft 66, a working partnership, on November 22, 1966. In the following years they successfully cleaned up in one competition after another. That the collaboration between Gerber and Lange, whom everyone always called Jimmy, would not be without problems was already apparent when the architectural office was named. Gerber describes the discussion of the naming: "Since I had graduated half a year after him, Jimmy argued that I should be named second, simply because of chronology; I argued that the names should be alphabetical, and finally won the argument." The cooperation between the two men remained difficult, leading them to soon dissolve the partnership. Beginning in 1968/69, each ran his own office. They collaborated only when working on large projects. But things changed once again when Dirk Stelljes joined the office, whom Gerber recruited directly from Braunschweig university in 1972. "Dirk Stelljes was congenial, open, and simply a great person. He came to us with his young wife and immediately built one of the terraced apartment buildings on the Lanfertsweg in Meschede, and he quickly found his place in the office as a partner. "For simplicity's sake, we reinstated

Founding of the Werkgemeinschaft 66 office in a basement in Meschede, Eckhard Gerber and Manfred Lange as newly graduated freelance architects in front of their first office in Hünenburgstraße 11, 1966

Jimmy as a partner in Werkgemeinschaft 66, and the three of us teamed up as equal partners in a GbR [a company constituted under civil law]. But even this constellation did not last long. "Differences in goals and in the management and development of our office were entirely different with Manfred Lange than with Dirk and me. Very difficult personal constellations developed, leading to Jimmy's departure from the partnership in 1974 and ultimately also to the separation from my first wife Anneli. Jimmy received a portion of the outstanding commissions from our office, especially the projects he had managed himself."

The first office of Werkgemeinschaft 66 was located in a basement room at Hünenburgstraße 11 in Meschede—a modest space that was just 2.25 meters high. "That was enough for our competition work." From today's perspective, however, the conditions under which young architects received commissions at the beginning of the seventies seem almost paradisaical. "With our university degrees as engineers, we could take part in any competition open to our region. Some competitions were open nationwide, others were open to certain federal states or even to certain government districts, counties, or cities." Usually, the partners focussed their efforts on their own region or the state of North Rhine-Westphalia. Only occasionally did they take part in nationwide competitions.

After ten years of independent work, Gerber took stock in clear terms, in black and white. The book he published—a nearly square volume, ninety-four pages long—gives an impression of the success his architectural practice achieved. It is a document of a moment in time and also an attempt at self-assurance. In addition to several residential buildings, Gerber, Lange and Stelljes carried out work across nearly the entire architectural spectrum: from administrative and office buildings to designs for churches and educational buildings, which would become a particular focus of Gerber's work in the following decades.

The primary school on Pappelallee in Lippstadt was built between 1967 and 1971 as a paragon of the brutalist exposed concrete style of those years. The design, with which Gerber and Lange won the first prize in 1968, loosely grouped the primary and special-needs school, as well as the sports buildings, around a central forum. But the young architects were quite frustrated when they only received the commission for the primary school. "Built externally and interally in lightweight structural concrete, the rough board formwork was precisely drafted in all perspectives. Even then, we learned that it was not possible to realize everything we designed and developed in detail. For

Volksbank Meschede, competition first prize, 1969•1972

Awarding of the Architecture Prize for Young Artists of the State of North Rhine-Westphalia by the NRW Minister of Culture, (*from left, front row*) Manfred Lange, Minister Jürgen Girgensohn, Eckhard Gerber, Dirk Stelljes, 1975

Samstag, 8. März 1975

Im Haus des Ministerpräsidenten in Düsseldorf übergab Kultusminister Girgensohn den Förderpreis des Landes an die Mescheder Architekten Manfred Lange (ganz links) sowie Dierk Stelljes (rechts) und Eckhard Gerber von der Werkgemeinschaft 66. WP-Foto: Zimmermann

Qualitätsvolles Bauen in der Landschaft verdient Anerkennung

instance, instead of our planned wooden windows, simple, cheaper aluminum windows were used." The restrooms spurred a particularly strange debate: "They should be planned separately for the Protestant and Catholic parts of the school. This was something I could not and did not want to understand, and eventually I combined the toilets together. Apparently the reason for separating them was to make sure they could be supervised by the respective religious authorities.

The construction of the school proved to be an enormous challenge for the new office, but it also reassured the architects about the path they had chosen. They had not yet gained any experience with a project of this size. It was thus a smart move for the newcomers to hire an employee with experience both in tendering projects and in managing construction to supervise the Lippstadt construction site.

From the mid-sixties onward, the Federal Republic of Germany had been undergoing profound upheaval. The years of the "economic miracle" of the immediate postwar period were replaced by a period of reflection and revolt in which the legacy of the parents' generation was called into question. The "summer of love" and the student riots left their mark, and Willy Brandt's epoch-making statement from his government declaration of October 1969—"We want to dare more democracy"—found its counterpart in a new start for the educational policies of the Federal Republic, which went hand in hand with a transformation of the educational system. New types of schools such as comprehensive schools and the founding of a number of new universities were signs of a new model in educational policy. This directly impacted architects, because new schools were built all across the country, and new universities were founded, from Bochum to Regensburg and Koblenz. The educational building boom in Germany that began then has never really come to an end. At most it lost steam for a few years, only to again pick up speed. But education was not the only thing that changed in this time. Architecture, too, underwent a fundamental transition in the 1960s. The change was visible in its forms, which became rougher and more cubic; in the material being used, which was increasingly dominated by exposed industrial concrete; and in production, in which the serial prefabrication of the components was coming to play an increasingly important role. The spectrum ranged from the British concrete Brutalism of Alison and Peter Smithson to the structuralism of Candilis, Josic, and Woods, whose urban designs resembled woven "carpet structures," and the early examples of high-tech architecture, with how they began to reflect on Archigram's

Primary school on Pappelallee in Lippstadt, competition first prize, 1967•1971

Primary school on Pappelallee
in Lippstadt, floor plan,
first upper storey

Primary school on Pappelallee
in Lippstadt, cross section

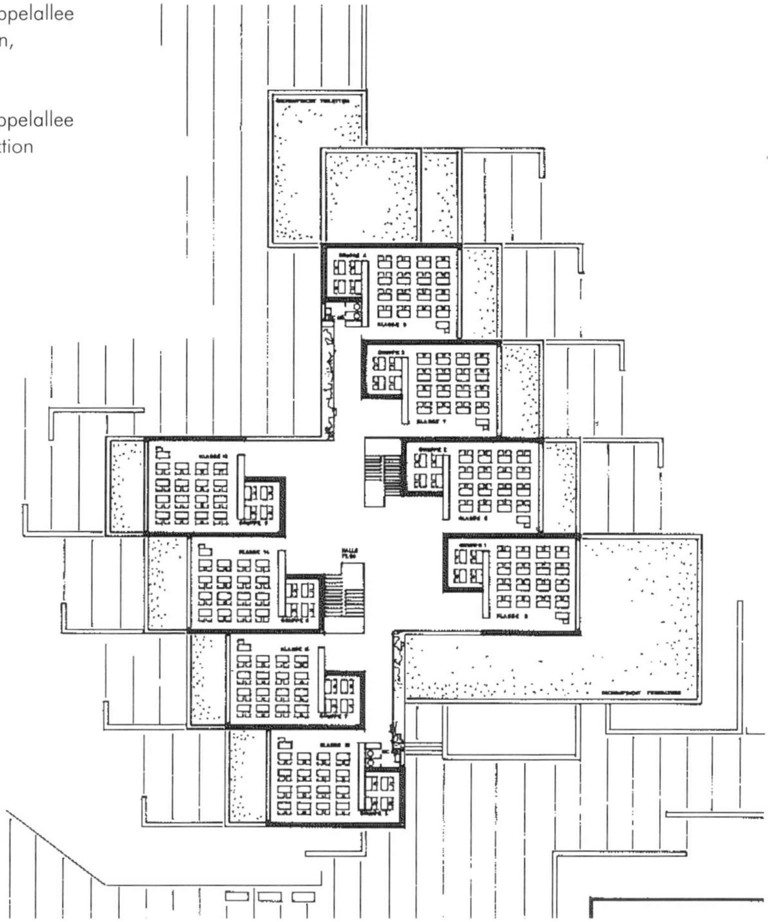

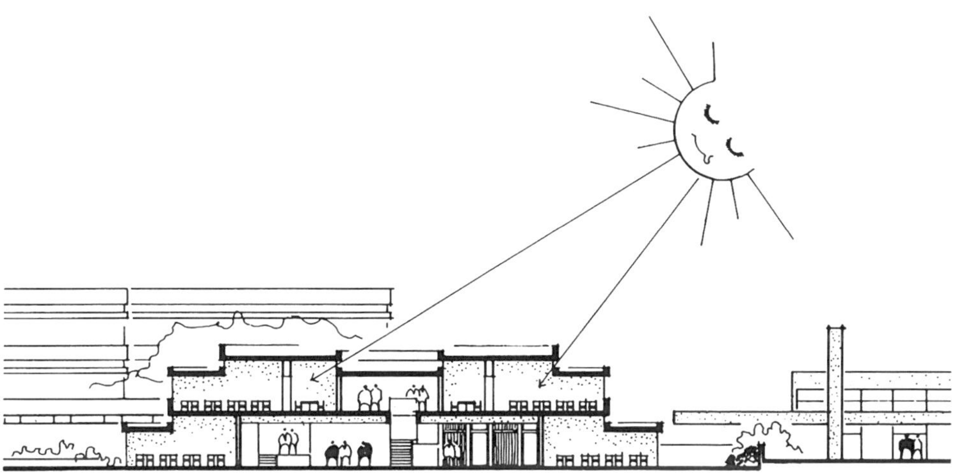

visions, or their realization by Norman Foster and Richard Rogers or, in Germany, by Günter Behnisch. Completely new attitudes and protagonists emerged on the international architectural stage, where they had a lasting impact—in some cases to the present day. In Sauerland, these developments were still far away. And yet the many school buildings that Gerber built early in his career, for example, exude an atmosphere energized by exposed concrete walls and wooden ceilings, similar to that which could be seen in the schools designed by Hermann Hertzberger in the Netherlands, whose work was close to structuralism. Indeed, the years of the early "Educational Republic" of Germany, as the political slogan ran, in which school after school was planned and built, proved to be an important impulse for the work of Werkgemeinschaft 66: they took part in an expert assessment for a grammar school in Winterberg (1967) and won commissions for a school center with a primary school and two types of secondary schools in Finnentrop (1968), and for another school center in Hamm-Uentrop, a secondary school in Bigge-Olsberg (1972–1974), and a secondary school in Meschede (1974). With each competition they won, the architects gained more experience; and with each building they realized, they also gained economic freedom, which they invested in order to bring their newly acquired experience to bear on new competitions. In the mid-seventies, up to nineteen employees were employed in their office in Meschede. But not all budding dreams became reality; not every competition was won, and not every competition they won was built. In addition to these successes, Gerber also experienced bitter disappointments. One of these great disappointments was the gigantic youth center in Fröndenberg. The project began promisingly for the partners. "I remember submitting our competition entry, which, of course, we did in person at the time. Jimmy and I handed in our plans and the model ten minutes before the deadline. The colleagues we encountered as we went in made a remark: "Well, now you're still happy." At first we didn't understand why they said this, but it became clear when we delivered our submission. We were the last ones to submit our entry, with a team number of 189."

Despite this fierce competition, the Werkgemeinschaft won the competition, which was open to architects in North-Rhine Westphalia. Their design, developed on a 60-degree grid, planned for the youth center to be grouped around a hexagonal square that was open on one side toward the countryside. "The idea was for the youth center to have a number of conference and seminar areas, as well as a sports and swimming hall, a large campsite in front, and rooms in which visitors to the center could stay. It was to become a loosely structured youth center, which the district administrator at the time, Jürgen Girgensohn, eagerly wanted to realize—probably in order to represent himself as an important politician within his party, the Social Democratic Party. The building's volumes, which were staggered in different heights, were planned to grow upwards from a common foundation. In its polygonal structure, the building's staggered volumes and floors—which appear to be layered horizontally—are reminiscent of Paul Schneider-Esleben's design for the Cologne-Bonn Airport. "The 60-degree grid was 'in' at the time," Gerber answers with a smile as I ask him about this similarity many years later. And Meinhard von Gerkan and Volkwin Marg, when designing Tegel airport in Berlin in the mid-sixties, did in fact rely on the same shape made of six triangles that Schneider-Esleben had also used. For statically constructive reasons, triangles are particularly pressure-resistant geometrical forms. Nevertheless, Gerber's project in Fröndenberg did not fare well: "We had been given the commission and had completed the construction documentation and the tenders. The construction sign was already hanging on the property, and we were about to award the contract to the construction company when the telephone rang: "The youth center is not being built! All the same, we as architects had entered into an entire contract with the district of Unna that included the construction management. We therefore received the total fee less services not rendered for the construction management of 40 percent. It was an architectural failure but provided us with a very good economic cushion. The project was scrapped because the idea of a comprehensive school came up at that very moment in time, and Girgensohn immediately switched gears and decided this kind of school was much more interesting because it was something new. Without further ado, he brought in the team of architects from Berlin who were responsible for the construction and planning of the new comprehensive school centers, designing the huge, highly controversial educational machines of which not a single one is left in the city today because they never really worked and nobody wanted to learn in them." But in life, you always end up meeting twice. This was also true for Girgensohn and Gerber. In 1974, during his tenure as Minister of Culture of North Rhine-Westphalia, Girgensohn awarded Gerber the State Art Prize for Architecture at the suggestion of Harald Deilmann. Once again, Gerber got to learn, in a nationwide competition, that neither winning a competition nor receiving a commission guaranteed that a building would be built. This commission also began promisingly. The partnership had since moved to a new office at Warsteiner Straße 7 in

Youth center in Fröndenberg, competition first prize, 1966, competition model, complete planning commission, not realized

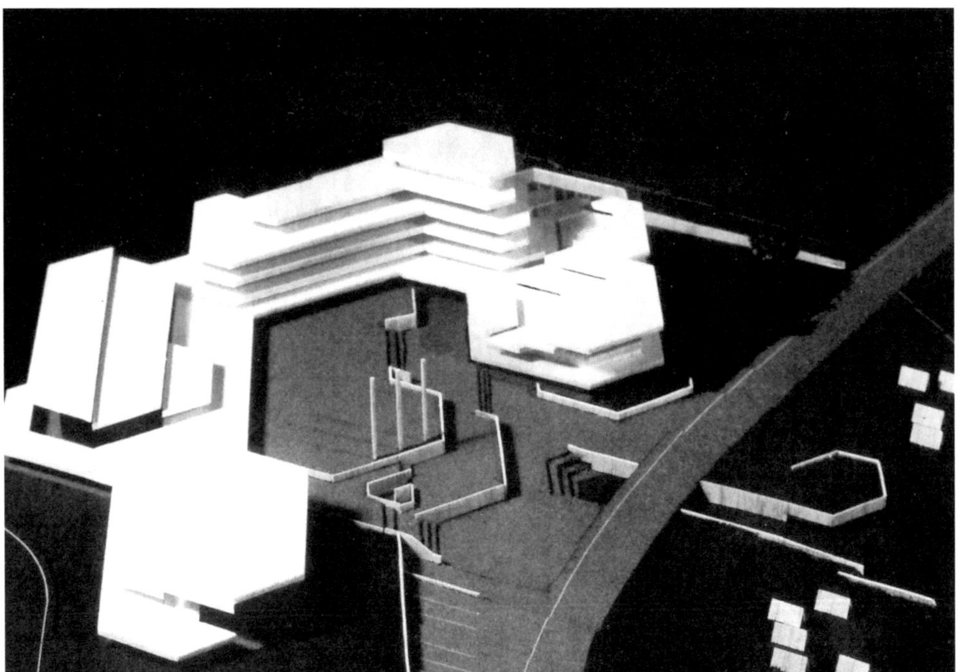

Meschede, when the office doorbell rang one evening. The entire jury of the competition for the Fachhochschule für Maschinenbau und Elektrotechnik (University of Applied Sciences for Mechanical and Electrical Engineering) in Meschede, which was meeting right in the city, had set out to deliver the happy news to the competition winner in person. "When I opened the door, the Chief Building Officer of the State of North Rhine-Westphalia at the time, Dr. Hallauer, was standing in front of me. He came up to me and said: 'Oh, you're Mr. Gerber, I remember your cheeky face well.' At my presentation of the report for the high school in Winterberg some time before, Hallauer had sat in the front row with the other judges. Coffee was served, and a young lady went around with one of the cans of condensed milk with two holes punctured in the top that were common at the time. Since the can was apparently still very full, and Dr. Hallauer was served first, the milk squirted out of the can in a high arc that landed on his pants. I couldn't hold back my laughter, which must have come across as a little cheeky. Perhaps this negative impression was the reason we had not been able to win the competition for the school in Winterberg." But the milk from that event was now water under the bridge, and we celebrated our success with the *Fachhochschule* by sharing a bottle of sparkling wine with the jury. This was an important contract for the office, requiring us to hire additional employees, including Dirk Stelljes. "We were in full planning mode when, on a Thursday before Easter week, we suddenly got a call from the Ministry in Düsseldorf that we should stop all planning work immediately. Economically, that was a huge blow for us. After all, we had assigned a large team to the project. I called all the staff together, and we worked around the clock over the weekend to quickly complete our 1:100 draft planning. The following Tuesday after Easter we informed the Ministry of our planning status." What had happened? The state parliament had passed a new law that required Gesamthochschulen, or comprehensive technical universities, to be founded as regular universities. The result was that various engineering schools were to be combined at one location. "Our engineering school for mechanical and electrical engineering was assigned to the University of Paderborn, and the Meschede location was to be abandoned." Werkgemeinschaft 66 was not the only architectural firm affected by the change in planning. At an event in Münster with almost five hundred participants, the concept for the new comprehensive colleges and universities in Paderborn, Siegen, Wuppertal, Essen, and Duisburg was explained to the offices, all of which were to be realized according to a precast concrete element system that had already been developed, and all of which

The first book publication by the Werkgemeinschaft 66 with the publishing house Wettbewerbe aktuell on the occasion of the office's tenth anniversary, 1976

Eckhard Gerber and Dirk Stelljes at their tenth anniversary celebration at Volksbank Meschede, 1976

The ten-year anniversary celebration at Volksbank Meschede, (*from left*) Prof. Harald Deilmann (keynote speaker), Herbert Böhme, Hagen city planning councilor, Eckhard Gerber, Undersecretary for North Rhine-Westphalia Dr. Fridolin Hallauer, 1976

were also realized except for the school in Duisburg. "This system had been developed by the Special Office for University Construction, which was headed by an architect named Dierksmüller in Münster. We were told that a master plan was available for all five locations specifying how the given structures were to be arranged at the respective locations. There were site plans with precise details for the placement of the individual areas. Most listeners were horrified by what they heard. "Some of our colleagues had tears in their eyes, fearing the demise of our profession. I tried to comfort everyone and explained with much optimism that this would not be the future for decades to come, but only a momentary decision that would change with the next shift in politics and personnel in the state of North Rhine-Westphalia." Gerber's assessment would prove correct. "The initiator of the entire prefabrication ideology was Hans Wertz, at the time Minister of Finance, who was very close to the construction industry. His intention was to produce prefabricated parts *en masse,* store them, and then take them from this stockpile to build up the individual complexes. This was meant to enable everything to be implemented as quickly as possible. But things didn't work out like this. Every project, every support, every beam, every component had to be sized accordingly and developed as a complete supporting structure. As before, the implementation was tied to normal planning. Hence, the advantage of prefabrication was—as it still is today—the possibility of completing the project more quickly on site, but with a correspondingly longer lead time in producing the parts to be fabricated." In order to realize the new universities, all of the architects who had been negatively impacted by this change in planning received a direct commission from this multi-billion mark building fund. In order to plan the individual locations, the architects were merged into groups. The impending economic disaster of the canceled commissions took a remarkable turn for Gerber: "We were grouped together with the office Bauturm, with Erich Schneider-Wessling and Peter Bussmann, as well as the architects Arlt and Philipp from Kreuztal." In an astute obituary written for Schneider-Wessling, who died in 2017, the architectural historian Wolfgang Pehnt concisely sketched out Schneider-Wessling's architectural stance, which is quite similar to that of Gerber: "The guiding concepts for his architecture were local reference, climate, appropriateness of means, community, the individual, modern technology, and nature. A notion of architecture that only considered form, as many of his colleagues today would undoubtedly elaborate, is not among them," Pehnt wrote. The team, which quickly formed a well-functioning

group, received the planning assignment for the Gesamthochschule-Universität Siegen. "Our task was not only to use a given system of precast concrete elements, but also the already developed building types. Each of these building types was a kind of longship, as it were, with conical, angular ends that lacked stairwells. The staircases were separate octagonal cylinders to which the ships, or blocks of buildings, were docked. Because of the conical shape of the ship's ends, a maximum of four further ships could be connected to one central octagonal core. These systems can still be seen at four locations today. The fifth site in Duisburg was no longer built according to this system after the project had been delayed due to difficulties with the approval of the development plan. My earlier assessment that this 'prefab madness' would be short-lived therefore turned out to be true." Gerber was especially impressed by Schneider-Wessling's negotiating skills. "Erich was a very likeable colleague who did not approach a project with a preconceived opinion, but deliberately left things open so that they could develop. This is how a process developed, especially in interactions with the client. This really impressed me. We drove together to our clients to Münster, and in addition to our presentation, we brought along a bag full of blocks. Erich then skilfully used the blocks to explain the design and make clear how it could be further developed: 'Look here,' he would say, 'this is what we planned, but we could do things this way or that way, too.' I've learned that this way of working was important for the success of a project, since it allowed the client to identify with the concept and accept it."
Thanks to Erich Schneider-Wessling's negotiating skills and creativity, the team of architects succeeded in replacing the strict urban master plan with their own concept, which also gave much better consideration to the strong topography. The plan was to develop as many areas of the building as possible in a "classic" way, while implementing only a few elements in the prescribed ship-tower concept. "In this cooperation, I learned a lot from Erich about how to negotiate skilfully and how to achieve success and quality for a building. Of course, we would have much rather preferred to realize our competition design for the *Fachhochschule* in Meschede. Especially since years later, Meschede was expanded as a satellite location of the Universität-Gesamthochschule Paderborn, meaning that our project could have been implemented without further ado."
Beginning in 1966, Gerber worked in Meschede for over a decade. Despite the setbacks with the youth center and the *Fachhochschule,* the decade turned out to be a good and productive one for him, during which he was able to

Fachhochschule Meschede,
competition first prize, 1971,
planning commission,
not realized

Gesamthochschule-Universität Siegen, architects Si-Planer, Erich Schneider-Wesseling (Bauturm Köln), Werkgemeinschaft 66, Eckhard Gerber, Dirk Stelljes, and Arlt+Philipp from Kreuztal, 1973•1976, replacement commission for the Fachhochschule Meschede

realize a number of projects, not least of all in Meschede itself. The most striking of these to date is his Volksbank (1969–1973), which also marked the start of other bank buildings he built, including the much later branches of the Volksbank in Dortmund (1999–2001) and Krefeld (2013–2015). The bank at the entrance to Meschede is characterized by a dualism of modernity and tradition, similar to that exemplified by Harald Deilmann in 1966 with his building for the Volkswohl-Bund insurance company in Münster. As an advisor to the bank and mentor to Gerber, Deilmann was one of the key backers of the project. Although the bank has unfortunately lost its original conciseness and generosity because of interior alterations, the effect of the exterior still remains. Yet Gerber decided to forgo a steep saddle roof in Meschede, as Deilmann had chosen in Münster. Instead, the Volkbank's striking, exposed-concrete stair tower, concrete columns, and horizontal window formats, which seem to have been carved out of the mass of the building, unmistakably appear to have originated from this moment in time. By dissolving the cubature of the building into an additive system of cubes, Gerber succeeded in integrating the building into the small-scale character of the site, while the violet slate cladding, with its traditional scaling, springs from the regional building tradition. The same sculptural quality of the design, the balance between rootedness in a place and innovation, characterizes other Gerber buildings from those years, such as the house he built for his parents at Plöner See, which stands amid traditional saddle- and hipped-roof houses. The deeply lowered roof with cut-out balcony openings, the unified exterior wall surface, and the striking chimney give the house a special character, clearly visible in its surroundings without upstaging the landscape.

On the outskirts of Meschede, we are welcomed by the Schäfer family, who have lived since 1971 in the bungalow that Gerber designed for them. The hillside location is deftly exploited, and the individual room compartments intelligently fit together, with the parent's bedroom on the living level and the children's rooms in the basement. The various views of the landscape, which extend as far as the Königsmünster Abbey, constitute a central element for the design of the wooden building. The house maintains a reserved stance outwards to the street while developing its special qualities inwardly and in dialogue with the landscape—not superficially, but in a way that is tailored to the needs and requirements of its residents, who have been very satisfied living here for nearly half a century.

In those years, the architectural partnership realized many detached, single-family homes. "Of course, word quickly got around in the small town of

Volksbank Dortmund,
competition first prize,
1998•2001

Volksbank Krefeld, competition
first prize, 2009•2015

Meschede that a young and successful architectural firm had settled here, so that we also received several direct commissions for residential buildings. One of these first commissions was for a two-family house in Oberdollendorf near Königswinter, located high on the mountain with a view into the Rhine valley, which was the home of my client, Dr. Donhuijsen, the chief physician of the Walburga Hospital in Meschede. Apart from the many competitions I sketched myself, it was practically my first and almost the only project for which I myself drew all the plans—all the design and execution plans, all the details, the front door, the windows, the interior doors, the cupboards, the furniture. For our office, that was a very nice, and very fundamental, project. For example, most of the details I developed for this house became the basis for our detail file, which we then also used for later projects. After the house was completed but before the handover, my client, Dr. Donhuijsen, invited me to inhabit the building for a day, and also to spend a night there. This was a beautiful, very personal, and friendly gesture that impressed me, as it was the first time that I had stayed and spent the night in a house I had planned myself."

For himself, Gerber designed a holiday home on Karerpass in South Tyrol, which was completed in 1978. "I built this semi-detached house, which we still cherish and love today, according to my plans together with my oldest brother, for both our families."

Yet it was not only in connection with the detached, single-family houses so common in the seventies, signs of the ample prosperity of the young Federal Republic, that Gerber engaged with the topic of building housing. He also engaged intensively with more dense forms of living that are still important today. "At the time, I was already of the opinion that areas with vegetation should be used as sparingly as possible, and, above all, that the areas and properties that should be built on are those not suitable for agricultural use. In the Sauerland, shaped by hills, this quickly led to considerations for terraced building types. Sustainability is not a new concept: sustainable building has always been one of the most important tasks for all builders throughout human history."

Internationally, many new paths were being pursued at the time for higher-density housing construction. In contrast to the desolate tenements that arose during the early phases of industrialization in the nineteenth century, the aim was for a high quality of living and a minimized use of land to complement each other. At the end of the sixties, the rigorous forms and materials of its exposed concrete had already made the Halen Estate near

Haus Dr. Donhuijsen, Oberdollendorf, 1967•1969

Gerber's father, Pastor Hans Gerber, with Gerber's mother, Emmy, in front of the family home at the Plöner See in Bosau, 1976

The Gerber family home at the Plöner See in Bosau, 1973

Schäfer residence, Walburgastraße,
Meschede, 1969

Vacation home at the Karerpass,
1976•1978

Bern, designed by the iconic Atelier 5, while in 1967 Moshe Safdie had caused a stir at the World Exhibition in Montreal, Canada, with a system of prefabricated concrete cubes. Its German counterpart, the Metastadt in the Neue Stadt Wulfen designed by Dietrich and Steigerwald, was a resounding failure and had to be demolished in 1987 due to vacancies and building defects. Meanwhile, between 1967 and 1973, Neave Brown realized the terrace houses of Alexandra Road Estate in Camden, London, which have received worldwide attention in recent years as an excellent example of high-density social housing. Gerber intensely engaged with all of these different living concepts, visiting buildings in which they were realized. Gerber's terrace houses in Meschede, built from 1969 to 1974, do not reach the dimensions of the London estate. They nevertheless offer a dense and yet also private form of living, staggered on a slope in a manner that cleverly heeds the topography. "This was a project I initiated myself, in which I operated with purchase options for the property, and which I was ultimately able to realize with a model in which the builders were also owners. I myself lacked the prerequisites to finance such a project as a whole. In total, the project includes five houses, each with three terraced apartments. I was looking for three builders for the first house, and when I had gotten them together, the first one decided to withdraw. So I entered the project myself as an investor. All costs for the subcontractors were negotiated, and I developed and determined the distribution of the shares myself, but with a notary, so that everyone, including myself, realized their own project in the form of condominiums with share allocations. When the invoices arrived, they were allocated and passed on to the builders for payment. The individual fittings for bathrooms, floors, and the like were paid for directly and not allocated among the builders." The building authorities in Meschede viewed the project with suspicion. The authorities believed that every owner in Sauerland would rather build their own house on their own property. But that was a fallacy. "After the frame of the first house was standing, demand for the other four houses was enormous." Even after he separated from his first wife Annelie, in 1974, Gerber and his two small children Nicola (born 1967) and Philipp (born 1969) remained in this house on the slope. This is not an easy situation for the freelance architect. He remarries in 1975. Two children result from this marriage with his second wife, Dorothee: Gero (born 1977) and Gesche (born 1979). Today, Gerber has been married to his wife Anngrit for twenty years. They have a son, Martin, born 2008.

The special atmosphere that must have prevailed at that time in the unusual, small residential complex in Meschede can still be felt at the friendly reception during our short visit forty-five years later. Rhythmized by the high towering chimneys, the alternation of sloping roof surfaces and terraces, and horizontal concrete bands and staircases, the three overlapping residential units of each building are at once skillfully nested and structured, comfortable and cozy, with materials and details typical of the time. "At first, the highest apartments were the most desirable, not the lowest ones, although it turned out that the apartments on the ground floor were the best to live in," which is something Gerber experienced in his own apartment with its beautiful garden.

Several times and on different scales, Gerber worked through variations of the theme of terraced houses in his designs, culminating in a large-scale study in 1967 for a hillside development on the Hünenburg in Meschede, which unfortunately remained only a project, as no investor was found for it. The residential development on Dinnendahlstraße in Essen, built fourty years later on the site, appears like a distant echo of this organic, small residential complex attached to the hillside. The long row of houses meanders up and down, with an effect that is both calming and moving, cozy and inviting like its older sibling but markedly different in its more austere, minimalist language.

Terraced houses on Lanfertsweg, Meschede, 1968•1974

Eckhard Gerber's apartment in a terraced house on Lanfertsweg, 1973

Habitat 67, Montreal World's Fair, Moshe Safdie, 1967

Hillside development on the Hünenburg, Meschede, 1967, study, not realized

Residential development,
Dinnendahlstraße, Essen,
competition first prize,
2004•2007

Rural Sparkasse and St. Petri church center, Soest, competition first prize, 1971•1974, competition model

Turning Points

Despite these internal tensions, the small partnership was quite successful. "An important competition success in this constellation of three architects, which lasted only a few years, was the rural Sparkasse in Soest, a beautiful concept, especially the work with the old structure, which was a medieval wall with foundations from a square residential tower. We won the competition, which was not only for a savings bank, but also a building for the St. Petri church community. Harald Deilmann was chairman of the jury and had described our work as a brilliant design. The project was located in the middle of the old town of Soest and its modernity was not uncontroversial." Beginning in 1974, a new chapter of the Werkgemeinschaft 66 began with a constellation of only two architects, Gerber and Stelljes. This collaboration marked a very busy and successful first phase of Gerber's independent architectural career.

Two special projects stand out: the Stadthalle or city hall in Hagen with an adjoining hotel, which won first prize in an architectural competition in 1974 and opened in 1981, and the Bildungszentrum der Bundesfinanzverwaltung (Training Center for the German Federal Reserve Administration) in Münster. Gerber won the first prize in 1976; no second prize was awarded. In 1987, the training center was able to start offering classes. Both were large projects that nevertheless differed clearly from each other in the type of building project as well as their architectural style.

Since the competition for the city hall in Hagen was only open to local architects, Gerber—who was from Dortmund—found a detour allowing him to enter. He applied together with his colleague Brettschneider (from Hagen), who, like Gerber, at that time also worked at the university in Dortmund at the institute of Harald Deilmann. But Gerber was in charge of the project from the beginning. A spectacular old quarry, which had been transformed into a large oval as the rock had been removed, was planned as the building site for the new town hall. "As always, I took a very close look at the local situation, visited several times, and engaged with the circumstances, and with the relationships between the paths and the views, in order to find a special solution."

While the other competition entries placed the city hall into the oval of the quarry, which is what the competition announcement called for, Gerber chose a different route. He wanted to leave the exciting rock oval of the quarry open and suggested it be used as leisure park: "This also coincided with my additional proposal to place the city hall at the end of the rock oval in order to make it visible from the city center and to create a visual relationship between the hall and the city. Realizing this overall solution, however, would entail blasting away around 40,000 cubic meters of rock. Since it was unclear what the costs would be, the jury, on which Gerber's former Braunschweig teacher Dieter Oesterlen also sat, initially awarded two first prizes. "Both offices were asked to examine their design in terms of cost. Since the blasting of the rocks alone would cost about one hundred marks per cubic meter, our design appeared too expensive." The rescue came from a good friend of Gerber's, who was managing director of a nearby quarry. "I asked him about blasting rocks in the quarry, since the stone couldn't be sold at such high prices. He told me this was relatively simple. They could blast away the rock for 5.50 marks a cubic meter. What mattered was that the stones not need to be transported anywhere, but could stay on the site. He then made me a binding offer for this blasting operation as a basis for the cost calculation of the city hall." Together with the revision of the planning, this calculation—in which the ground blasting cost only 220,000 marks instead of four million—tipped the scales in favor of Gerber's design. Since the blasted boulders had to remain on the site to avoid expensive transport costs, the idea arose to use the stones to shape the landscape and develop a rock garden designed by the landscape planner Georg Penker. However, the implementation of the project dragged on, as the construction of city halls in the mid-1970s met with political resistance from the municipalities because of the later maintenance costs they entailed. "Böhme, a very clever and energetic man and head of the city planning office in charge of the building, formed a team of four with the mayor at the time, Loskand, the town director, Müller, and the treasurer, Dr. Pesch, who absolutely wanted to build the city hall. It was to be a multipurpose hall with primary use as a concert hall. We therefore had to find a way to get the project underway so that there would be no turning back. I convinced Böhme that it would make sense to begin by blasting away the rock, which would be necessary in any case. We wouldn't have to waste effort boring thirty meters into the rock but could make boreholes that were much shorter. He liked my idea, and the rocky outcrop was blown up by my friend's quarry company."

Hence, the largest obstacle—in the truest sense of the word—that was preventing the city hall from being realized was cleared away. Now the large cavity in the rocks had become a reality, and the city came under pressure to realize the project. "As with other projects we realized, we opportunely used the available window of time, which was often only very short. During

Hagen city hall in the quarry, on the street Wasserloses Tal, competition first prize, 1974•1981, model

Hagen city hall in the quarry, on the street Wasserloses Tal, 1974•1981, aerial photo

Hagen city hall in the quarry,
on the street Wasserloses Tal,
1974•1981

the implementation, it was particularly important to me to highlight the contrast between the solid rock and the brittle, smooth, crystalline glass surfaces of the hall," says Gerber, explaining the design concept for the city hall. Brown with shimmering silver, the rocks in front of the steep slope blend into the landscape and small park that completes the city hall ensemble. The rocky ground from which the airy, glass hall rises continues as a decorative stone ensemble into the foyer of the building. In Hagen, the landscape and—once again, with Gerber's characteristic touch—the sensitively staggered architecture merge together. The result is a composition displaying both transparency and mass, lightness and weight, in which the open and closed spaces intermesh and the green coloring of the closed wall surfaces and glass frames blends into the surrounding trees, which by now have grown into a dense grove. From the covered entrance of the city hall, visitors are led via the high central foyer, amply supplied with daylight and with changing views of the city center, into the rock oval and the large and small event halls, which can be outfitted with chairs and used in various ways. Polygonal in its basic sixty-degree structure, the ceiling of the large hall is supported by a wide-span steel construction that emphasizes the technical character of the house and thus brings a bit of high-tech ambiance to the late-Jugendstil city. Intensively used, the restaurant has not retained its original design, and the bowling alley has since gone out of fashion and disappeared. Gerber later replaced these spaces with a simple, multifunctional hall. What has remained is the overall impression of the hall, with its airy concrete and steel construction marking an effective counterpoint to the natural stone environment. It is a typical building of the time, not only highly functional and with a distinctive design, but also with heritage value after almost forty years, despite some unattractive conversions and additions that appear to have sprouted like weeds, without reducing the high quality of the overall effect. This level of quality also extended to the detail of the building's flexible seating, which was chosen during a trip to Italy, near Bologna. Gerber chose the Vertebra chair system developed in 1977 by the Argentinian-American designer Emilio Ambasz and his Italian colleague Giancarlo Piretti, which Castelli marketed in Europe. The construction of the adjoining hotel, which was the element of Gerber's design that dominated vertically, took an unfortunate course. Since the city did not want to be responsible for the construction, it gave the property to a private hotelier. "He had his own design developed that didn't fit in any way into the overall concept developed in the competition. I complained about this to Loskand, the mayor, telling him this was intolerable." After traveling with the hotelier to visit three of the man's properties, Gerber developed a new design concept for him. "The hotelier looked at the plans and the model and announced fifteen minutes later: 'I am going to build this design!' I was thrilled. But then he finished his sentence: 'But with my architect.' That nearly left me speechless, because I had never in fact encountered such a situation before, although such a request is unfortunately often made today. We therefore agreed that I would work out the preliminary design but that further planning would then be carried out by his architect in consultation with me. Unfortunately, however, the hotel was only partially developed on the basis of the preliminary draft."

The ground plan of the city hall is based on structuralist designs. But at the same time the wide glass surfaces already suggest motifs from Gerber's later buildings, as one finds in the wonderfully bright Universitätsbibliothek in Göttingen and the wide hall of the Mitteldeutscher Rundfunk, whose front provides a view of the Magdeburg city center. Along Gerber's path to constructing these buildings, the segmented structure still evident in the project in Hagen is increasingly pushed back in favor of a greater sense of calm. When asked about the direction in which his architectural development should go after Hagen and Münster, Gerber answers quickly and confidently: "Toward reduction. I've found people always want too much." Gerber's architecture did in fact tend toward greater reduction the following years, but without becoming minimalist. At the same time, it appears more pointed in formulating contrasts, which develop a formal and material tension with the respective basic cubic design forms.

At the nationwide competition for the Bildungszentrum der Bundesfinanzverwaltung in Münster in 1976, Gerber was able to outperform both Harald Deilmann and the students from Hamburg with whom he had studied in Braunschweig, von Gerkan, Marg and Partners. At first glance, the formal difference between the city hall in Hagen and the training center, built only a bit later, could hardly be greater. Both are public buildings. But while the hall in Hagen is distinguisehd by its transparency, the building in Münster stands directly across from a massive ensemble of red brick masonry overgrown with earth—a typical Westphalian phenomenon. With this building at the very latest, it becomes clear that one will look in vain in Eckhard Gerber's works for a salient artistic style or signature imposed on all of his projects in the way that had become fashionable for many architectural brands from that time. With Gerber, the connections are subtler, less obvious, yet still present. They draw nourishment from Gerber's approach to a construction task, and thus come instead from an attitude that seeks the right, appropriate solution. This solution always incorporates the location and its topography, in the same way as it does the respective construction task, and it additionally pursues the goal of creating something more in spatial terms than what was actually demanded in the tender. This "more" refers not least of all to the quality of communal spaces, to foyers, and corridors; it is not only that people enjoy spending time in these spaces, but also that the spaces enable additional use for informal encounters, for communicating with others, or just for a short stay. Because this is what architecture is all about, and this is Gerber's signature: creating spaces that open up an additional dimension, as a matter of course, beyond the expected and familiar, which is something we as users then also take for granted. What the city hall in Hagen and the training center in Münster have in common is this structural approach of optimally solving a given construction task and also creating spaces with added value. Of course, the usual cost discussions for all projects—especially of this size—also followed for the project in Münster, with the result that the number of rooms and total surface area were reduced. In addition, there was also a threat that one of the concept's central ideas would be lost, namely, the passage of the residential wings leading from the square into the open landscape. "The architect in the Regional Financial Office in Münster who was in charge of the project was able realistically gauge what the department in the Ministry of Construction in Bonn would and would not approve. I wanted to preserve the passage, which was an essential basic idea of the concept, and so I proposed to build colonnades on the ground floor of the residential wing in order to maintain the intended connection from the street Gescherweg via the central square into the open landscape. We were thus finally awarded the contract, but only for the design and construction documentation, as well as the artistic supervision, and not for the tender and construction management, which the Federal Building Office preferred to retain itself," Gerber recalls. When all the difficulties seemed to have been overcome, the project suddenly faced the same fate as the Fröndenberg Jugendzentrum and the *Fachhochschule* in Meschede. "On the day of the contract negotiations for the shell construction, a call came during the negotiating round not to award the contract for the time being. Instead, it was to be examined whether this project could be realized in Schleswig-Holstein. The reason was a change in the Ministry of Finance in Bonn. Gerhard Stoltenberg from Schleswig-Holstein had become the new Minister of Finance in 1982 and preferred to see this project in his state. It was wise that the project manager had already put a lot of preliminary work into this project, for the

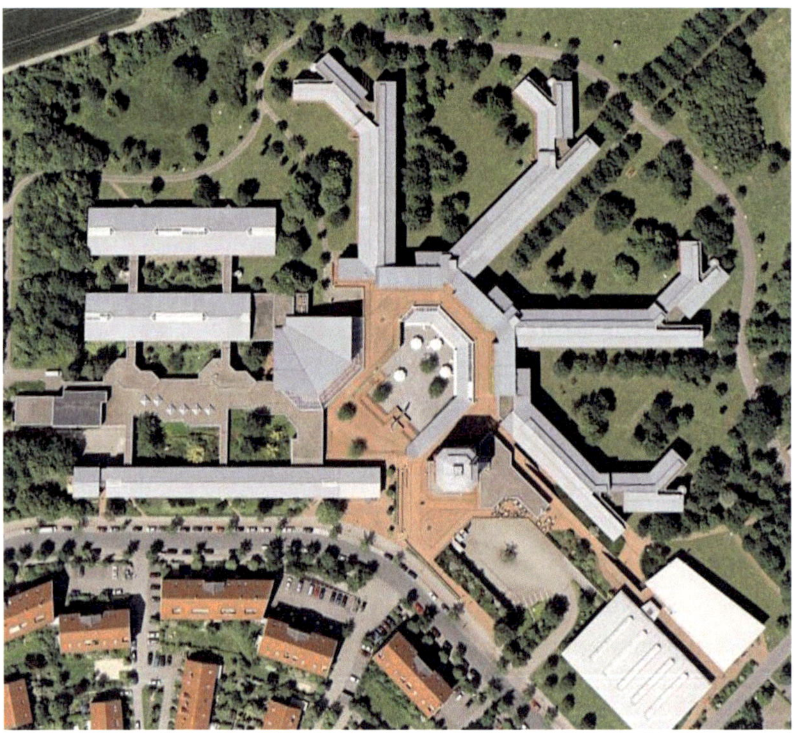

Bildungs- und Wissenschafts-zentrum der Bundesfinanzver-waltung, competition first prize, 1975, competition model

Realized from the perspective of an aerial photo

Bildungs- und Wirtschaftszentrum
der Bundesfinanzverwaltung,
Gescherweg in Münster,
1975•1987

sewers, drainage, construction roads, and earthworks, thus opportunely using the time window available." When a compilation of project data showed that more than ten million marks had already been invested in preparing the project in Münster, the relocation to Schleswig-Holstein was off the table. "It was obviously no longer politically justifiable to accept such a substantial amount as lost costs for the project and choose a new location." After an interruption of nearly six months, the project was finally officially started. "The initially distrustful project manager and staff member from the State Building Department in Münster, Mr. Götze, gradually become a trusted friend who highly valued my work. He was an experienced project manager who had seen it all. He was one of the few representatives from this public client who really did have construction experience across the entire planning and construction process, who was pragmatic and willing to take on responsibility. For example, it became necessary to shrink the size of the artificial lake that was part of the site. He agreed to this change, doing nothing more than fill up the lake with less water so that its total area became smaller."

For the further planning of the grounds, Gerber involved the office of Georg Penker, as he had done in Hagen. "[Penker] supplemented the colonnades with a powerful avenue of trees, which was a great idea," Gerber says, underscoring Penker's contribution. "Today, after thirty years, the high quality of these open spaces is evident now that the trees have reached their appropriate size. But we planned the paved central square ourselves because I viewed it as a direct part of the architectural concept."

If you look at the floor plan of the training center in Münster, what stands out is how structuralist it is. In addition, the design with pent roofs and brick walls exhibits references to the Scandinavian architecture of someone like Alvar Aalto. But today, Gerber is quite critical of his own work: "Münster is an example of where we still wanted too much and, unfortunately, far too many people had a say. When it was finished after more than eleven years of planning and construction, there were lots of things that I didn't like anymore. In terms of the ground plan and the conceptual idea, it was and still is coherent. But in its formal elaboration the building is not as clear and simple as I imagine architecture today." Like a small town, the buildings in Münster are grouped around a central, polygonal courtyard, around which they meander in height and distance. At the entrance of this forum stands the bronze sculpture *Matthäusbrücke* (Matthias Bridge) by the sculptor Eberhard Linke: it thematizes the history of the apostle Matthew, the patron saint of tax collectors. Its upward swing forming the arch of the bridge introduces visitors both thematically and spatially to the training center. A residential tower for the lecturers forms a small, dominating tower, and the communal facilities form the heart of the complex: the open courtyard, the covered hall, the cafeteria that nestles around the courtyard, the large classroom and—last but not least—the library. With its two different heights, joined by steps as well as columns illuminated from above, it also exudes Scandinavian airiness. Lit laterally through a high glass front, the small library already prefigures the much larger university library in Göttingen, one of the major works in Gerber's oeuvre. Behind the extensive courtyard development, four residential wings with the trainees' apartments reach into the landscape like fingers. These residential wings are bent on one side at their end. In this way, they create an anchor point in the environment; they don't become lost in their vast surroundings but reach into the landscape like finger tips, visually delimiting the space. On their reverse side, with their colonnades and an accompanying avenue of trees, they display two further motifs that Gerber successfully employed to enclose the space.

Despite such timeless compositional principles, the training center in Münster is interwoven with its time. A row of turquoise tiles on the floor marks the gap between the brick floor and the brick walls and the round supports painted by Pitt Moog. The doors to the side wings are framed by bricks in the shape of bottles and give the impression that they are crowned by a broken pediment. The postmodernity of the eighties is winking just around the corner. Since then, Gerber has also developed a critical distance to these kinds of details, as he reports during our long evening conversation at the Tönnishof, Gerber's home and the nucleus of his Dortmund office, which will still be covered in detail: "The brick was and is right for this project, right for a building in Münsterland, and it is a very sustainable material, so that today, after thirty years, the complex looks almost like new. This is true in general for northern Germany, such as in our projects in Hamburg, the housing we designed in Wilhelmsburg, and the media campus in Finkenau. I also believe that decoration and ornamentation will certainly play a role in architecture again. But in Münster, the turquoise tiles on the floor, which touch the edges of the walls and columns, as well as the stepped arches of the colonnades, are too much a product of their time. Today, for me, that has more of an arts-and-crafts echo."

But it's also surprising for me to see how the two buildings in Wilhelmsburg and Münster, which were built at quite different times, thirty years apart, are joined together, beyond the pure material of the brick, by a kindred look and feel. Gerber nods and agrees this is the case, while nevertheless adding that "Wilhelmsburg and the media campus are much further along," which is certainly true both formally and chronologically.

A game with postmodern motifs is also evident in his own addition to the residential villa of the Tönnishof Estate, from 1985. "I saw the architectural language of the addition more as persiflage," he admits. "The farce wasn't meant seriously. But everyone took it at face value. Probably for this reason, it had received a lot of attention at the time, including in international publications, also appearing on the front pages of several professional journals." Indeed, the kind of postmodern motifs characterizing the renovation and expansion of the adjacent stable and barn building into an architectural studio, which was completed in 2004, might not be expected to come from an otherwise consistently staunch modernist such as Gerber. Connected to the old building of the residential villa by a glass staircase, Gerber's transversely aligned residential extension of the manor house appears as a rectangle from which geometrical forms have been carved out, opening like a moon gate toward the garden. The building and the landscape glide into each other. Some architects who build a house for themselves reveal a piece of their own soul, often won with difficulty after a long inner struggle. "But that's exactly what I didn't want," Gerber confesses as we continue to immerse ourselves in his architectural and private biography in conversation, and a small mountain of books and project documentation piles up before us. The playful extension of his residential house with its closed walls and striking openings appears in brilliant white. "I was afraid that everyone would say: 'Aha, so this is how he's building things now,' and the clients who might come to visit us would think: 'Now I can have something like that, too!' But they won't get it! Maybe I was making things more complicated than they needed to be," he says as he smiles. I nod, equally happy about the false trail he left for potential clients with his house. "Adlo Rossi and Charles Moore are smiling at your extension of the Tönnishof," I say, trying to situate the rather unusual house in the context of Gerber's work. "Maybe," he says a little mischievously, "if they could still smile."

Tönnishof in Dortmund-Kley, extension to the residence, photo 1986

Tönnishof in Dortmund-Kley with parts of the original farmyard from 1884, photo 2018

Design Principles

Eight years after founding his own architectural practice in 1974, Gerber was offered a position as a correction assistant with Harald Deilmann at the Universität Dortmund. This enabled him to combine the work in his own office with teaching. Deilmann was one of the central figures of postwar modernism in northwestern Germany, and his works also show "organic" architectural impulses from southern Germany, reflective of his studies with Rolf Gutbrod in Stuttgart and his teaching in Baden-Württemberg (from 1964 to 1969). In addition to his office in Münster, Deilmann also operated another office in Stuttgart. While his brutalist high-rise for the Volkswohl-Bund insurance company in Dortmund was unfortunately demolished, his striking West-LB building continues to define the city center. His activity as a teacher has also shaped architectural discourse in Dortmund since 1969. It was in this context that he developed the "Dortmund model." This curriculum allowed students to combine architecture with experience in the construction industry and structural design, and hence to network different competences. In addition to Deilmann, the engineer Stephan Polónyi, the architect Hans-Busso von Busse and later also Josef Paul Kleihues were also involved in developing the Dortmund model. After his time with Deilmann, Gerber initially received a teaching position at the Universität-Gesamthochschule Essen (University of Essen) in the early 1980s, which led to a professorship in the following year in the field of "fundamentals of design and applied design theory for architects and landscape architects." Gerber confesses: "I have always been very connected with teaching and have consistently pursued teaching opportunities since opening my office. It started with my slide collection, which I immediately began to build up. For me, the chair of architecture and landscape architecture gave me the impetus, on the one hand, to deal more intensively with the topic of landscape design and, on the other, to consider what didactic content would make sense for the students on the subject of the fundamentals of design." Gerber derived the didactic concept he then developed from two very different experiences of his own. On the one hand, there was his knowledge, always connected with the open questions that had arisen from his practical work as an architect. And on the other hand, he remembered well the time of his own training with Kraemer and Oesterlen in Braunschweig and the many questions that had arisen as he was designing, and which none of his university teachers could answer satisfactorily. "I didn't know at the time how to come up with the form and shape of a design. Nobody was able to properly tell us, or teach us, how to do this. Oesterlen taught us how to build and how to win a competition with an extraordinary idea. He also taught us how to approach a task from a design point of view. But nobody taught us how to find form and shape. So I asked myself: 'Are the fundamentals of design and engineering even teachable? And if so, what's the best way to get them across?'" Gerber's goal for his didactic concept was to give his students all the tools they needed for a good design already during their studies, the very tools that he had had to develop himself with a lot of effort. "Anyone can have an ingenious idea for a building by chance. But this is far from the skill of working out long-lasting solutions for a wide variety of construction tasks," he says with conviction. "Anyone who has ever worked in teaching knows the challenge of independently developing a curriculum. Part of this process is to critically question one's own experiences, one's own knowledge. "Before beginning to teach, you are first of all occupied with analyzing and with getting to know yourself. The aim is to question your own positions with regard to their viability and to try to order them and integrate them into a large structure. This is no easy undertaking. However, this critical reflection on your own actions broadens your own horizon and enables you to communicate your own positions to the students in a way that can be understood." For Gerber, too, teaching offered a fantastic opportunity of this kind: "The subject 'fundamentals of design' was good for me insofar as it was the subject I knew the least about. The teaching forced me to go deep into the topic, and I learned quite a lot myself, which in turn became important for our own work beginning in the 80s." Gerber's teaching in Essen led to a position in Wuppertal in the 90s, where he taught "fundamentals of design and applied design theory." And he in turn felt that this change was a boon for himself "because it represented a further development." Even after his official retirement in 2004, he was still involved in teaching, and he continued his commitment to project development in the master's program. Two years ago, he was also offered two guest professorships, in Harbin and Dalian in China, each of which he takes up for a period of time twice a year.

Gerber's didactic concept was based on two cornerstones. On the one hand, it enabled the students to analyze and learn from existing buildings. And on the other hand, it enabled the students to develop the form and shape of their designs themselves on the basis of the principles they learned. Of course, the concept does not replace the idea required for a design, the creative impetus, the urban planning, or the functional and technical necessities. These must be developed in parallel. Rather, the concept is understood as a way of finding a design based on a theory of form and composition. This concept also expresses Gerber's very structural way of thinking. In this respect, his teaching concept is about nothing less than a description of the fundamentals of architecture and their effect. But what are these basic principles? The task of architects is to develop spaces: 'When a client comes to us, he wants us to build a building; he wants spaces in which people either live or work, a library, for example, or a university, and so on." But every space is always more than just a simple room. Spaces have a specific atmosphere and thus engender moods and sensitivities in their users. "Every space affects our sensitivity. It's not possible to withdraw from spaces because they surround us all of our lives. Whether we are at home or in kindergarten, going to school or later studying or working—we are always surrounded by spaces, even urban spaces and landscapes. These spaces can make us cheerful, happy, joyful, sad, some can even make us even aggressive." In this respect, architecture in general is hugely important, for individual buildings and for urban space, in its effect on individuals who live or work in these spaces or pass by them every day. Architecture affects society as a whole and its state of mind. For Gerber, one central aspect of a degree in architecture was thus that teachers teach their students to be "steadfast in fighting for good architecture and to learn how to communicate this to their clients. To make their clients understand that they have an obligation to the public. Even before architecture is designed and built, it therefore poses a question of responsibility—toward both clients and society. Gerber divides his teaching into clear steps that proceed from a building to the city. Each building is an enclosed space with openings through which one enters and leaves, into which natural light penetrates and through which one can look out into the surroundings. The shell and its surroundings stand in a direct relationship to each other, regardless of whether the building is situated in the countryside as part of a landscape or in the city. There is always interaction between a building and its surroundings. "This is where architecture begins, because from the very beginnings of architecture, buildings have always been about the connection from inside to outside and from outside to inside. The addition of individual buildings produces urban spaces, and the arrangement or grouping of buildings produces streets and squares." The shells surrounding these spaces are the sequences of inner walls and outer façades, and it is their design that we have to deal with intensively. The effect of a square is determined by the façades of the adjacent houses, but the character of a square is also defined by the design of its surface, which in turn results from its specific functions. For example, what good is the most beautiful square if its drainage doesn't work? "The basis for designing any square is thus its drainage. The best examples of this are the squares in Siena and Capitol Square in Rome. And then we turn to the individual building, which I divide into three structures: primary, secondary, and tertiary. The load-bearing primary structure is the shell, which can consist of wood, steel, stone, or concrete. This is followed by the non-load-bearing secondary structure, which is the shell that surrounds a building skeleton (the primary structure) or the openings in load-bearing wall surfaces (the primary structure), which can be closed by non-load-bearing window elements or used to shape a load-bearing skeletal structure. This secondary structure is necessary in order to close off the building climatically, and it usually consists of glass, wood, or metal surfaces as nonbearing shells or shell parts. The tertiary structure completes this division. The tertiary structure is also non-load-bearing and includes interior fittings such as (non-load-bearing) walls, stairs, or interior cabinetry elements. While the secondary and tertiary structures are comparatively easy to change, the primary structure, as the supporting structure of a building, is difficult or impossible to change." For Gerber, the primary structure represents the DNA of a building, as it were. So far, so good. But this is hardly enough to design any building. "As a student, I once thought about how to design a kindergarten. So I got myself magazines and studied already-existing designs for beautiful kindergartens, perhaps two of which I really liked. My kindergarten could be like this or like that, I thought to myself. But that's not a good approach for a design, because it means you are only working on something that already exists. It is much better to penetrate into the original basic structures of the form and shape of a building and thus develop one's designs in a new and unique way." For this process, Gerber invokes four design principles. The first is the principle of a cube as a self-supporting, closed volume, but with openings. "The surface proportion of the window openings should of course be considerably smaller than that of the closed load-bearing surfaces, since this makes the cube principle that much stronger. The second design principle is the frame. It can be derived from the cube principle, resulting when this supporting framework is reduced to a minimum by maximum openings, meaning the cube is ultimately reduced to supports and beams. Here, for example, extensive infilling between the supports and beams would be necessary to provide a climate shell (secondary structure) or a secondary envelope. The third design principle is the wall principle. This principle is also derived from a cube, from which only the walls are taken and placed loosely in relation to

Piazza del Campidoglio, Rome

Piazza del Campo, Siena

each other. The fourth principle is that of the floating roof, which closes the cube upwards and dominates the design to such a degree that the necessary vertical supports recede into the background."

These four design principles are joined by five forms: the three geometric forms of the rectangle, the circle, and the triangle; and two free forms, namely the curved forms derived from the circle and the bent forms derived from the triangle. "If I work through these five forms and the four design principles together, I get a considerable range of design possibilities for a design, in the way Ludwig Mies van der Rohe, for instance, always worked, even if he never directly talked or wrote about this process.

Seen in these terms, Gottfried Böhm's pilgrimage church in Neviges, in massive exposed concrete, was developed from the cube principle with a freely folded form, while the Romanesque church of St. Michael in Hildesheim was also developed from the cube principle, but with the addition of cylinders, square towers, pyramids, and cones. The framework principle, by contrast, is used in structures such as half-timbered buildings, as well as the "skin and bone buildings" of modernism, such as the famous Seagram Building in New York where Mies used it paradigmatically.

"Werner Sobek's house, with its visible filigree steel skeleton, enabling maximum transparency, is also based on the framework principle and on right angles, derived from the shape of the square. But one can also use a curved framework, as can be seen in the example of the Olympic Stadium in Beijing designed by Herzog and de Meuron." Here, too, Mies represents the floating roof principle with his Neue Nationalgalerie (New National Gallery) in Berlin, and also the wall principle with his Barcelona Pavilion. "On the basis of the wall principle, it can be demonstrated how flowing spaces can be created through limitation and openness, with interesting pathways inside and outside. The Barcelona Pavilion is based on the design principle of a rectangular wall, as is the Versöhnungskirche in Dachau, where the principle of a wall was declined through a series of freely folded forms. Another reason these two buildings possess a completely different character is the differences in their materialities. Yet both projects, the Barcelona Pavilion and the Versöhnungskirche in Dachau, rest upon the design principle of the wall. These principles can thus be used to analyze all of architecture, to understand the thinking behind its design." The principles can be found in their pure form less frequently; an example is Mario Botta's early residential tower Casa Bianchi as a pure expression of the cubic principle. Instead, we usually find combinations: "the four design principles in combinations with the five forms, which already produce a wealth of design possibilities. But the four principles can also be linked together: wall and floating roof, for example, or cube and frame, or one can transition from a cube to a frame. A classic example is the work of the New York architect Richard Meier. Meier linked all of the design principles together and articulated them in various forms, thereby developing his buildings into built sculptures. And in order to ensure that these many different things would cohere, he colored everything white.

To this day, Gerber receives positive feedback from former students on his way of teaching design principles. He supplemented this theoretical approach with the requirement that his students produce compact designs. "In three weeks, everything had to be ready from start to finish, or at most, sometimes it was six weeks. All of the students were given space in one room, twelve to fifteen of them. I came by almost every day, usually after working in the office, and sometimes late at night or on the weekends, to discuss and correct the work. The draft designs thus took shape in a very short period of time. It was important for the students to work together, because the exchange of ideas and discussion among themselves allowed them to develop and learn independently." But how was it possible for Gerber to combine this time-consuming work at the university, which was accompanied by intensive supervision of the students, with the management of a successful architectural office? It was possible only because Gerber turned many nights into days. "At the university, I gave lectures and offered seminars on two days during the week. Late afternoons was when I then corrected student work. The rest of my time was reserved for the office. I only realized how much work it was when I stopped doing it," he explains with a smile in his office at Tönnishof. "But all this was and still is only possible with a team of outstanding employees and partners who, like me, contribute to the work on our projects with joy, enormous energy, and a high level of commitment.

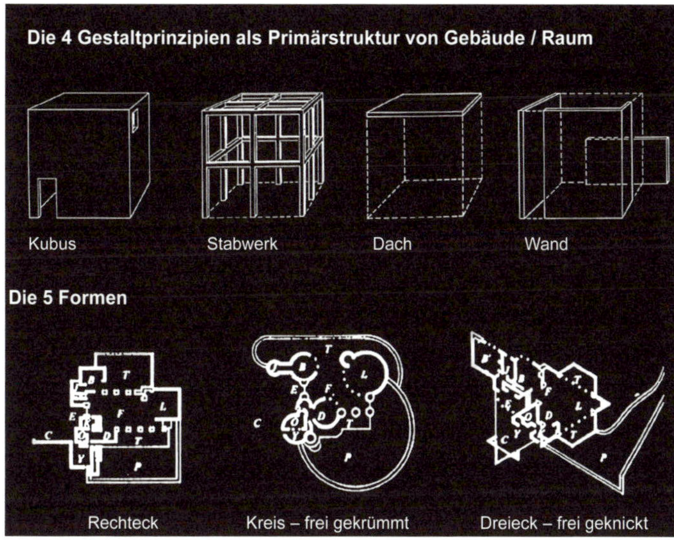

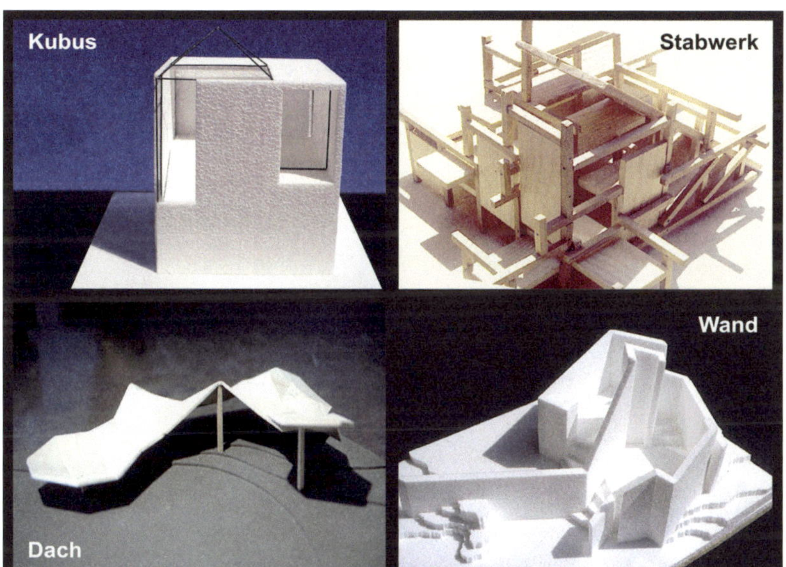

The four design principles and five forms

The four design principles and five forms, student practice exercises

Taking Off in Dortmund

Dortmund Central Station and Tönnishof in Dortmund-Kley, the site already mentioned here several times, are about a quarter of an hour apart via the S-Bahn line 1, just five stops. And it's only a three-minute walk along the railway embankment, framed by tall trees, to get to the estate. The former residential villa lies on the left side of a roundabout on a small piece of woodland, with the former barn to the right: the house where Eckhard Gerber lives and where his architectural firm, Gerber Architekten, is located. The highway A40 is not far away, which leads from the Dutch border via Duisburg, Essen, and Bochum across the Ruhr district to Dortmund and, in its extension as A44, onward to Kassel. Dortmund has been synonymous with coal, steel, and beer for so long that one almost forgets its earlier history as a member of the Hanseatic league, and that more than a thousand years of history and commerce are rooted here in Westphalia. Structural changes in its economy have meant that coal, steel, and beer have survived only as the city's history and stories. What has remained, apart from the soccer club Borussia, are fragments of meaning scattered by the wind. In their place, new symbols have become manifest, signs of a new urban identity. Some of them catch your eye right upon arriving at the Dortmund Central Station. First, there are the unequal siblings, the Harenberg high-rise and RWE Tower. And then, of course, the Dortmunder U, always radiantly golden, shining above the city atop the brewery's seventy-meter-high former fermentation and storage cellar, at the base of which the campus of the Robert-Bosch-Berufskolleg (Robert Bosch Vocational College) is located. All of these are projects developed by Gerber Architekten over the last twenty-five years. In the postwar period, Dortmund was shaped by the work of Will Schwarz with his Florianturm (Florian Tower, 1958/59), his Parkcafé in the Westfalenpark (1959), and especially his magnificent Gesundheitshaus (House of Health, 1955 to 1959). But over the last three decades, Eckhard Gerber's buildings have begun to mark the city.

The Tönnishof has been Gerber's home since 1979, the beginning of his time in Dortmund. It functions as both a workshop and place of retreat. Were the years Gerber spent in Meschede just growing pains? Or did they create the technical and financial tools necessary for Gerber to take the next step? And why did he come Dortmund? Why not Münster, where Harald Deilmann's office was located? Why not the state capital of Düsseldorf, where state politics played out? Or even further afield to Berlin, where, for example, the Westphalian-born architect Josef Paul Kleihues moved after his studies in Stuttgart? Together with his partner Dirk Stelljes, Gerber agreed in 1978 to establish a second office in Dortmund. After a decade in Meschede, the Westphalian province no longer held any potential for Gerber. "It became clear to me that in Meschede I could not continue building the kind of architectural office I envisioned. The city and the region were simply too small and insignificant. That's why I decided to move the office." The office opened in Dortmund on January 1, 1979. The original plan was for Dirk Stelljes to continue working in the office in Meschede. But this was prevented by a traffic accident that took Stelljes's life at the end of 1978. "So I decided to give up the office in Meschede altogether and move everything to Dortmund." The planned expansion of the architectural office became a completely new start, especially since most employees didn't want to take such an uncertain step in moving to Dortmund and stayed in Meschede. The work began in Dortmund with six employees. "Only two employees came from Meschede at the time."

Did Gerber have any idea then that, forty years later, with around one hundred and eighty employees, he would be running one of the largest architectural firms in Germany? In addition to the new opportunities that the larger city offered, which Gerber also quickly pursued, there were pragmatic reasons for the move. "The move to Dortmund became economically feasible only because of the project in Münster. We won the competition in 1976, and two years later we were awarded the contract. At the same time, we were working on the project for the city hall in Hagen, which opened in 1981, and a vocational school center in Lüdenscheid. This meant I was constantly driving to the area anyway, so it made sense to just move there." Nonetheless, the move to Dortmund also entailed risks given dramatic structural change that was taking place in the city and region. At the end of the seventies Dortmund was marked by the decline of the triad of coal, iron, and beer that had formed the economic foundation of the city for nearly a century. At the same time, however, this decline was the seed of the structural change and remarkable regeneration of the entire region, which found exemplary expression with the IBA Emscher Park built between 1989 and 1999. This process was initiated by the urban planner Karl Ganser and Christoph Zöpel, a politician serving at the time as Minister for Urban and Regional Development in North Rhine-Westphalia. To this day, the decade that saw the construction of the IBA Emscher Park stands as a sign of the outstanding importance that architecture, landscape, and urban planning can play in transforming a region if only they are carried out wisely, and

Dortmund with vocational colleges lower left, Dortmunder U, Harenberg City Center and RWE Tower, aerial photo 2018

of the role that this transformation can play in the mentality and mood of the population, which is not something that should be underestimated. For Gerber, the decision to move to Dortmund at the end of the seventies therefore brought together a number of different aspects. These also included connections between architecture and business that were particularly evident in city, and that were not unimportant to him as an independent architect. It mattered to him that "extraordinary businessmen such as Alfred Herrhausen, who came from Essen, or Detlev Rohwedder, the CEO of Hoesch who promoted the Ruhr area" also lived in the city. And the Tönnishof? "When I decided to go to Dortmund and asked the city for a suitable property, they offered me the estate with the manor house, which at the time was not in a good condition, completely dilapidated. The long brick stable block, which we later converted into our office, was still being used by a riding club at that time. The farmer living here had sold his land after the newly built S-Bahn line had cut off his four-sided farm from his fields. The city then bought the twenty-five hectares and converted them into an industrial park. With the proceeds, the farmer could then buy ten times the land in Schleswig-Holstein and build a new farm," Gerber says, cheerfully describing his move Dortmund. The old residential villa, built in 1884, is marked by pilasters and a portico that bespeak the late classical prosperity of the important farmer who once lived here. In the wide foyer there are paintings on the walls that became visible during Gerber's renovation as newer layers of paint were removed. From the beginning, living and working were organized together at the Tönnishof under one roof. "We transformed the attic of the residential villa into the office, while the ground floor was left unchanged, though renovated and used for the secretarial office and meeting rooms. We lived on the middle floor, to which we added an extension in 1985 so that we could use the entire old building for the office and live in the new building."

With its success, the office continued to grow. "Later we had to rent more rooms, because there was simply not enough space before we moved to the Harenberg building (which we designed) in 1993." Meanwhile, the residential villa remained an office. This is where most of the competitions in which the office participated were designed and drawn. Twenty years passed before Gerber had the opportunity to acquire the adjacent long stable building. "In 2004, we were able to move into the former stables, which we converted into an office. That allowed us to locate the construction management department in the old residential villa, which is also where our Chinese projects will be supervised in the future."

As in Meschede, most of the projects in Dortmund came from competitions held for public clients. "The only way we could get contracts to build was through competitions, because when I started out working for myself, I was a former refugee from the GDR and lacked any networks that might provide me with direct commissions. Over time, however, as his success grew, more and more private clients turned directly to Gerber. This is also how his two tallest, cityscape-defining buildings in Dortmund, the Harenberg Tower and the RWE Tower, were built, but some time would pass before then. Gerber's first building in Dortmund was a smaller sibling to the city hall in Hagen, the city rail stop at the Stadtgarten (City Garden). Dramatically destroyed in the Second World War, Dortmund is a city shaped by reconstruction, especially in its center, where it boasts several outstanding works of architecture, most notably the headquarters for the city's health administration built by Will Schwarz. Nonetheless, Dortmund still remains a city with brittle charm, and its expansion and reconstruction are far from complete. Yet this brittleness is not only a consequence of the destruction the city suffered in the war but is also connected with the structural change the city experienced, during which the large areas in the city center of the Thier brewery and the Dortmund-Union brewery fell out of use. Dortmund has thus remained a city of permanent transformation, marked by civic pride and a search for itself, architecturally and culturally—open to the new but always at risk of being content with mediocrity. The city rail stop came out of one of these urban reconstruction/new building projects. It was part of a competition for urban planning ideas that also included the area around the Stadtgarten, which was laid out in 1982 on the southern edge of the former city embankments, as well as a new city hall. "Our design envisaged a slow transition from the landscape of the Stadtgarten to the urban space of Dortmund's city core. We first received the commission for the city rail stop." However, while the stop was being built, there was another competition for the new city hall, which was no longer to be built at the same location as envisioned in Gerber's urban design. This second competition produced the cubic monolith of the new city hall, located on Friedensplatz and built according to a design by Dieter Kälberer. With its pink natural stone façade, the building appears to be somewhat lost in the urban space, a late testimony of postmodernism and, for Dortmund, a wasted opportunity to develop a larger, coherent urban landscape at this site. Gerber's city rail stop, reminiscent of a glass chinoiserie, is something else entirely: a greenhouse in the park that modulates the topography of its surroundings. The extensive red brick walls of the rail stop connect with the topography and landscape; they were extended via a stairway to join with the fountain designed by Eberhard Linke, creating a symbiotic unity of building, landscape, and artwork. Linke's fountain of jesters uses the gradient of the terrain down to the city. Its water cascades into the basin made of the same red bricks that forms the circular fountain with bronze figures. The flowing water rounds off the shapes of the rail stop located higher up the incline.

Again and again, as I engage with Eckhard Gerber's buildings, I am tempted to think of them in musical terms. The city rail stop is a prelude, a bit foreign. But its combination of two design principles, wall and roof, marks it as a last link to Gerber's time in Meschede, and as something different from his later buildings in the city. This project was followed by the duet of the two tower buildings, the Harenberg high-rise and the RWE Tower, to then become the trio of the Dortmunder U, the adjacent schools, and the Harenberg high-rise, and eventually develop into a polyphonic symphony of Gerber's works in Dortmund. Is this impression just a playful metaphor derived from Gerber's love of music? An arbitrary analogy? I think not, because we could also turn to the concepts of syntax, or phrase construction. Of course, Gerber's buildings in Dortmund were built independently of each other. In the democratically created world of a city, no architect can impose their signature alone. Which is a fortunate thing. Because a city always entails changing forms and layers of time; it always means diversity. That's why continued development in the city also always means engaging with what already exists, and thinking about context. Eckhard Gerber's buildings integrate this spatial context into their design to a special degree, in terms of both architecture and the landscape. They develop this context further, while also extending it by providing new accents, a sound of its own. This happens on multiple levels: in an architectural language of forms that is resolutely bound to modernism; in its intensive design of gardens and landscapes, in the city and in the countryside; and in its outstanding creative accentuation. These three aspects are internally related; they form a magic triangle and develop a new inner harmony with each project, as is evident, for instance, in the employment office that Gerber designed in Dortmund. The office was built on the outskirts of the Nordstadt district, directly across from the Central Railway Station and in proximity to the Harenberg high-rise and the RWE Tower. This was a building site with which Gerber was familiar from a previous competition for an adjoining communication center; in that competition in 1976, his design of a far-reaching structure of a "flying" roof intended to join

Tönnishof, Dortmund-Kley
after the Second World War,
photo 1949

Tönnishof, Dortmund-Kley,
farm 1984, photo 1906

Tönnishof, Dortmund-Kley, residential villa from 1884, following restoration 1978•1979

Tönnishof, Dortmund-Kley, aerial photo 2018

together the space and its various functions only won second place. "Even today, I try to take part in the colloquia for an architectural competition myself, if possible, so that I can hear things—sometimes very important things—said between the lines. Sometimes, these supposed trivialities are not even recorded in the minutes. This was exactly the case in the competition for the Dortmund employment office, open to architects across the state. The client made an offhand remark that interior courtyards were not particularly valued. We thus developed a concept with two large wings that ran parallel to Steinstraße and Fürstenstraße and framed the property on two sides. In the park-like open space created at the rear, we placed a separate building for the Berufsinformationszentrum (Vocational Information Center), or BIZ. I wanted to make it possible to open a pathway through the building from the Central Station to the north. The pathway should cut through the employment office, without resulting in a functional separation in the building's different floors. That's why we excavated the lot by one storey and modulated it so that one can walk up an outside staircase under the building coming from the Steinstraße. On the ground floor and the upper floors, a glass bridge construction creates an inner connection between both parts of the building. The connection in front of the outside staircase that goes beneath the building was located in the basement floor. I had seen a similar concept at the Rem Koolhaas Museum in Rotterdam and was very interested. In that building, Koolhaas had managed to penetrate the space with a long ramp from the lower to the upper level. James Stirling also achieved such a result in his Staatsgalerie in Stuttgart, designing the public pathway to lead through the open courtyard of sculptures that is surrounded by the museum. The construction for the winning competition design for the employment office from 1988, which I worked on with Jürgen Friedemann at the time, lasted until 1995. The excavation created level areas for the canteen and other spaces on the basement floor oriented toward the beautiful park." With the mostly closed, perforated façade facing the city and the delicate glass façade facing the park, the building has two very different faces. Where the two wings meet, a small public square is formed by a setback—a gesture to receive visitors, but also to wave them through. The building is characterized by an atrium, flooded with bright natural light, spanning its entire height with a sculptural staircase. It is filled with museum-quality art. Immediately behind the entrance, one finds a wall segment with a large-format work by Emil Schumacher, the important representative of German Informalism. It is done entirely in white, blue, and black. The nat-

City rail stop Stadtgarten, Dortmund, competition first prize, 1978•1982

Heinz-Bach-Haus, Continentale Versicherungsverbund, Dortmund, competition first prize, 1983•1987

ural color of the large tuff blocks of the wall shimmers out from under the colored glaze, fired in a Bavarian workshop. Schumacher, who was born in Hagen, had previously been slated to contribute a work for Hagen's city hall, upon the recommendation of the city council. But the project foundered because of the inappropriate and inadequate way in which the city's Building and Arts Committee treated the artist. In Dortmund, Eckhard Gerber now had a new opportunity to launch a collaboration, this time with success. Together with Schumacher's work, two kinetic objects by George Rickey are also on display. When Gerber visited Rickey, whose studio was temporarily in Berlin, the artist made it clear: "If they want something from me, they better hurry up. I'm already old." But he had plenty of creative energy left for the two works in Dortmund. Rickey died in 2002, three years after Emil Schumacher.

In the twilight of a late winter afternoon, Eckhard Gerber and I stand in one of the upper floors of the Harenberg high-rise. Through the mighty windows of the building we look out at Dortmund, after a long day of sightseeing and good conversations. The city literally lies at our feet: the huge area of the Central Station, which city planners had once dreamed of covering over, together with its tracks; to the right of the station the historic city center with its three principle churches St. Reinoldi, St. Marien, and St. Petri. The city center and railway station are separated by the wide strip of the Königswall, or King's Embankment, a section of the wide road built where the city fortifications once stood; Mario Botta's beautiful city library pushes outward into the street, as does the museum of the German Football Association (which is unfortunate, since the building is much too large and boxy). From this vantage point, the RWE Tower seems to look at us directly with its prominent upper floors, which crown it like a brow. Completed in 2005, it comes across as the big sibling of the Harenberg high-rise and as a brilliant counterpart to the Botta Library across the street. It's hard to believe, but true: at first glance, you don't realize that the two buildings were designed by the same architect. They are separated by almost exactly ten years. The first time I came to the Harenberg high-rise was in 1997, for a meeting with Eckhard Gerber, who had rented office space in "his" high-rise until 2002, until he could concentrate his entire Dortmund office at the Tönnishof. When I asked him if he could remember our conversation from then, he shakes his head with a sad smile. "No, what did we talk about?" As an architecture journalist who had just finished his PhD, I was currently working on a documentation of the federal government's buildings in Berlin

Agentur für Arbeit Dortmund,
competition first prize,
1988•1995

that were created when the government and parliament moved to the city. Gerber nods: "At the time, we designed the conversion of the old building for the Federal Ministry of Construction, and now I can remember our conversation." The former Prussian Geological Office and Mining Academy on the Invalidenstraße in Berlin had, since 1945, been part of what was popularly called the Kleine Museumsinsel, or Little Museum Island, which also included the nearby Natural History Museum. The complex was designed at the end of the nineteenth century by one of Schinkel's successors, August Tiede. For its new use as a ministry, the building had been cleared of the inner construction that had been carried out by the GDR; the beautiful atrium was once again opened up. Gerber had found a highly structural solution, typical of his designs, for the building's offices. He imposed a smaller, second room structure consisting of steel columns and wall elements over the tidy historical system of rooms in the original building. The solution was equally sensitive and remarkable in its treatment of the existing building, even if I personally wasn't able at the time to situate the design in the context of Gerber's complete oeuvre. But luckily, in life you always end up meeting (at least) twice. Even then, on my first visit, I was impressed by the nineteen-storey Harenberg tower, which has become a city landmark with the powerful clarity of its concrete grid, especially on its delicate narrow side, just four windows wide, facing the railway station. The texture of the concrete grid finds a counterpoint in the building nicknamed a "slice of cake," with its round lecture hall, and in the glass staircase rising from the foyer on the inner-city side. This white steel staircase gives the building a technical note. Looking from the railway and the Nordstadt upon the wide breast of the high-rise, one notices two wider strips of concrete on each side, enclosing smaller-scale windows. "Of course, my intention was for the façade to be gridded evenly, but that's not what the client wanted because it increased costs for fire protection." As much as Eckhard Gerber's wish makes sense to me, I cannot escape this accentuation of the house on both sides, which only makes the rest of the grid stronger, emphasizing it and saving it from the threat of monotony. After almost thirty years, however, the question urgently arises of whether this building ought not be given the protection of historic preservation, before the first wave of redevelopment sweeps by. The danger exists given changes in the owners and tenants. The entrance and cloakroom area, located in front of the steeply rising, round event hall, has already been reshaped. The hall itself retains its original form and is waiting to be awakened again with a kiss, to come alive with readings

Agentur für Arbeit Dortmund,
1988•1995, atrium

Dortmund Hbf
F
F
Dortmund Hbf

RWE Tower, Dortmund,
2002•2005

RWE Tower, Dortmund,
bistro on the top floor

RWE Tower, Dortmund,
groundbreaking on
December 9, 2003,
(*from left*) Eckhard Gerber,
Martin Dreier, Mayor
Dr. Gerhard Langemeyer,
Erich Dreier Sr.

and lectures and world-class concerts, such as those once organized by the original client, the publisher Bodo Harenberg. In order to arrive at his high-rise publishing house, Harenberg—known for publishing the beautiful series *Die Bibliophilen Taschenbücher* (Bibliophile pocketbooks) among other things—commissioned three designs. The building site was a former tram loop, which was initially to be replaced by an urban block. In the eighties, postmodernism was in full bloom in Germany. In addition to Gerber, as Harenberg reports, the two postmodern old masters, the Austrian Hans Hollein and the Italian Aldo Rossi, provided designs. "But he wanted something to be created that was as neutral and raw as a factory building, so reduced in its qualities that it could not influence the making of books, which Harenberg also saw as works of art."

Harenberg City Center, Dortmund, 1989•1994

At the beginning of the nineties, Gerber sought out contact with the investor Erich Dreier. In his role as chairman of the Dortmunder Kunstverein (Dortmund Art Association), Gerber made an effort at the time, using a study, to win over the successful local real estate entrepreneur for the project of an exhibition building for the association. But Erich Dreier senior had other plans. The Kunstverein, which is now located in the Dortmunder U building, did not get its own building. But for Gerber the conversation with the senior Erich Dreier was the prelude to a successful collaboration and later close friendship with Dreier's sons, Martin and the junior Erich, which also gave rise in 2003 to the project development for Gerber's second high-rise in Dortmund, the RWE Tower that was completed in 2005 and bears the name of its first tenant. The RWE Tower truly looks like an antipode to the Harenberg building, which is a decade older. Instead of a cubic form with a rough exposed concrete façade, the RWE Tower is dressed in dark granite slabs on its façade, curving elegantly to form the shape of an oval ship. Both the position of the building in the urban landscape and its prominent, brow-like upper floors, which thrust the building upward to the southeast, are unusual at first glance. What closely links the two buildings is the way in which they are derived from the urban context of their surroundings. Taking a look with Google Earth is helpful here: while the slender Harenberg high-rise building nestles closely to the railway on its narrow lot, the swing of the REW Tower responds to the semi-circular funnel of Mario Botta's municipal library that has been drawing attention in the city since 1999. Like a joint, the RWE Tower creates a transition to the Museumsgasse with the Museum für Kunst- und Kulturgeschichte (Museum of Art and Cultural History) and its entrance, formed by a concave colonnade and a convex

façade that prefigures, as it were, the Tower's geometric idea. At the same time, the high-rise proves to be a conscious urban planning intervention of its own: "I always liked the way the Catholic court church of Gaetano Chiaveri in Dresden diagonally pushes into the city plan and thus defines new spaces," Gerber confesses. As in nearly all of his buildings, Gerber found a way to offer added use value in the RWE Tower in both the exhibition space in the ground floor and the building's top floors, where a cafeteria for the employees is located. The room is impressively dynamic, drawing its energy from the interplay of the upward surge of the outwardly curved wall and the rhythm of the vertical window openings. The wonderful view out across the city, beyond its edges, amplifies this spatial quality. Eckhard Gerber remembers the reaction of Dreier, who had also become a friend: "'It's a good thing I didn't realize the design would create such a high, empty space here,' Martin Dreier said when we were first up here together in the unfinished shell." "'Had I known, I wouldn't have built it. But now I'm glad it's turned out like this.'"

Looking over from the RWE Tower to the Harenberg high-rise, one sees the massive brick tower of the Dortmunder U. The U from which the building takes its name sits atop the tower like a crown. It has been become so tightly bound up with Dortmund's self-understanding and self-confidence that it almost seems to be a piece of the city. This U was not even originally part of the brewery tower. And yet that's sometimes how it is with landmarks: over time they accrue a meaning of their own—a meaning that assumes a life of its own and goe far beyond the original message. And this is what happened with the U that has crowned the tower since 1968 and the identity it has given the city. It was designed by Ernst Neufert, one of the most enigmatic and strident German architectural figures of the twentieth century. Born in 1900, he was an early Bauhaus student, wrote a "theory of building design" (1936) that has remained fundamental to this day, carried out research into possibilities of industrializing and rationalizing construction, became deeply entangled in the Nazi regime as an employee of the war criminal Albert Speer, and, after 1945, built several exceptional new buildings, such as the Eternit main factory in Leimen and the single men's hostel in Darmstadt, where he also held a professorship. The U, with its mighty substructures in the tower, stood at the end of his architectural career and ultimately also at the end of the brewery chapter in Dortmund's history. The brewery tower itself was built in 1926/27 as the fermentation and storage cellar of the Dortmunder Union Brewery. It was designed by the Dortmund engineer and architect Emil Moog. Moog placed a red brick shell around the pure concrete construction that constituted the functional building, in which the brewing process took place from top to bottom, following the force of gravity.

After the brewery was moved elsewhere in 1994, the city of Dortmund bought the former industrial site in 2007. At the time, a first wave of ideas for new uses had already rolled over the site, without any architectural consequences. Even before the move, in 1993, the brewery company that owned the site, the Brau- und Brunnen AG, had launched an urban-planning ideas competition. The British designer Richard Rogers emerged as the winner, despite the fact that his high-tech designs had never found much success in Germany. In Dortmund, too, he would come up short. "The time wasn't yet right for the site," Gerber explains in retrospect. He himself had also participated in the competition. His design, in which he had already envisioned a cultural use for the U, as well as the construction of a adjacent concert hall, had been recognized by the jury with a special mention. After the brewery was abandoned, the area was cleared out right up to the mighty tower, which initially stood unused and empty. In retrospect, the Dortmunder U seems a bit like a metaphor for the entire city: a potential problem child and future space in one. There were major political disputes over the preservation or demolition of this monument, so important for Dortmund. When the Ruhr area applied to be a 2010 European Capital of Culture, a breakthrough occurred with the decision to transform the Dortmunder U into a center for art and creativity. In addition to cultural institutions, the plan called for the university to use space in the building, too. In 2006, Gerber Architekten and Gernot Schulz won the limited architectural competition that was held to design the transformation. "At the time, we thought a lot about what the right idea for the house might be until, after intensive studies, an idea hit me like a lightning bolt: we would cut a swath along the east wall through all of the building's floors, thereby making the huge space in the city also come alive on the inside—simply by having a joint cut into it. We then worked with a colleague, Professor Pfeifer, who was a structural engineer, to clarify whether this was even possible. He assured us: "It is!" The result is spectacular: a tremendous gash through the entire building makes clear the structure's dimensions and allows all floors to be centrally accessed by escalators leading up to the space called the Cathedral, the topmost section of the tower that Gerber's design envisions as spectacular event venue. The publicly accessible roof terrace offers a special added value. On the match

Dortmunder U—Zentrum für Kunst und Kreativität, 2006•2010, Kunstvertikale (art vertical)

Dortmunder U—Zentrum für Kunst und Kreativität, competition second prize (no first prize was awarded), 2006•2010

Inauguration of the Dortmunder U—Zentrum für Kunst und Kreativität, (*from left*) Minister President of North Rhine-Westphalia, Jürgen Rüttgers, Dortmund Mayor Ullrich Sierau, Eckhard Gerber, 2010

Vocational college, Dortmund, competition first prize, 2011 • 2016, with the Dortmunder U

days of Dortmund's soccer club Borussia, the vantage point not only offers a close-up encounter with Adolf Winkelmann's video installation, which features the club's players in their black and yellow uniforms. The view of the city is also impressive. The ground floor of the Dortmunder U has space for a restaurant, cinema, and exhibition areas, while halfway up the building a newly built balcony of glass juts out of the old brick shell and opens up above the city, looking in and out. It forms a special exhibition space as part of the city's Museum Ostwall, now housed on the fourth and fifth floors of the tower. Anyone walking in the evenings from the train station to Reinoldikirche will consistently encounter the video installation, shining through the night like a friendly alien that quickly becomes familiar and tells us something about how immensely important Gerber's revival and reinterpretation of the former brewery tower has been for the city. The relocation of Brinkhoffstraße, already envisioned in Richard Rogers's plan, has resulted in a new square in front of the building. Even if it does not perfectly connect the cultural complex with the city center and the train station, it still creates some space and, with it, desirable area to carry out actitivies. Another of Gerber's buildings stands behind the tower: the brick-red vocational colleges, built from 2013 to 2015 and developed by Gerber together with Benni Sieber and Jens Haake in a PPP process. They laterally enclose a central square that functions as an open campus. Beneath the rising benches, which invite visitors to linger but are also intended as a grandstand, the college's large auditorium has been tucked away, sunk into the ground and, characteristic of Gerber's designs, supplied with daylight from the side and from the rear.

Building Education

Laments about education, complaints about the decline of knowledge (and what is taught at school), and pleas for reform have been a sign of high culture since antiquity. It's no wonder, then, that Germany, the land of "poets and thinkers," has seen one wave of reform after another. This tradition goes back at least five hundred years to the time of Philipp Melanchthon, the friend of Martin Luther's who was honored as "praeceptor germaniae," "teacher of the Germans." How significant was it, then, really when a *Bildungsnotstand* or "education emergency" was declared fifty years ago in the Federal Republic of Germany? The term was coined by Georg Picht, a philosopher and educator. In 1964, he published a brilliant plea in the newspaper *Christ und Welt* (Christ and the world): "One foundation of every modern state is its education system. Nobody ought to know that better than the Germans. The rise of Germany to join the circle of great cultural nations was founded in the nineteenth century by the expansion of universities and schools." In some regards, Picht's admonition does in fact prove to be surprisingly current, for example, when he states: "In our modern 'meritocracy,' social justice means nothing other than the equitable distribution of educational opportunities, because these are the basis for social advancement and the distribution of income. Picht's proclamation of an education emergency was like the proverbial straw that broke the camel's back, triggering a wave of reforms at schools and universities. The shock triggered by the Pisa report on the state of European education in 2001 thus had a notable precursor. What all these educational efforts had in common was an urgent need for new spaces. Although the construction of schools had already been an issue in the classical modernism of the Weimar Republic, it was by no means a point of focus. Things were different in the postwar period, when architects explored fascinating new forms of schools in their designs for pavilion schools—most notably, Hans Scharoun with his two, recently renovated, schools in Marl and Lünen. Even in the sixties, the demand for schools did not abate, producing models of reform schools that fundamentally differed from their predecessors in their clearly anti-authoritarian pedagogy. Alongside these many new schools, a number of new universities also emerged, with the consequence that higher education lost the elite status it had previously held. In line with Picht's view, education was understood to be an important resource for a society that was losing parts of its industrial character. From the sixties onward, this was especially true for regions like the Ruhr district. The many new universities founded at the time, such as those in Dortmund, Bochum, Essen, Wuppertal, and Hagen, were an essential prerequisite for the economic restructuring that was necessary for the region. Education policy thus became one part of the response to structural change in the Federal Republic of Germany. The increasing political and sociological coloration of educational discourse also had an effect on architecture. Not only were more and more new schools and universities being built, but new spatial structures were also being formulated, aimed at fostering a greater sense of community and lowering thresholds for teacher-student interaction. This "education emergency" in the Federal Republic of Germany was followed by an educational awakening, with all its trials and tribulations. The founding of the Werkgemeinschaft 66 in Meschede and its participation in so many competitions for new schools thus coincided with this time of optimism and renewal in education. Some of these, such as the school in Lippstadt, were won and realized. Although the Werkgemeinschaft had already participated in building a postsecondary school with the university in Siegen (albeit via several involuntary detours), and the training center in Münster represented a comparable task, not until the 1990s did the firm Gerber Architekten come to focus on the entire spectrum of educational buildings, from university buildings to a range of research institutes and the most challenging and prominent of tasks, university libraries. For Eckhard Gerber, the success in these competitions of recent years stems from several factors: "Of course, it always takes a bit of luck to win a competition. After all, there is never only one good solution. But once you have carried out a commission for a university and established a good point of reference, it becomes much easier in today's competitive world to be invited at all to participate in a competition, and even to win from time to time. This has always been very difficult for young architects, and today it is especially the case. When we started out back then, we were able to take part in any statewide or national competition, in contrast to how things are today. Building for universities is particularly important to me because I have always considered teaching to be important. In addition, many universities are not located in urban settings but in newly developed areas, providing more scenic surroundings. This is a boon for our approach to design, which is always especially attuned to the landscape." Projects such as the city hall in Hagen, the training center in Münster, the library in Göttingen and the first building for a research institute designed by Gerber, which was completed in 1997 for the Leuphana Universität Lüneburg, show how Gerber directly integrates the landscape into his design practice. "At the opening for the institute, I stunned the audience by explaining that the building had been developed based on the concept of a Black Forest house." Its location on a hill allows for the rear side of the machine hall in the upper floor to be approached at ground level, while the front side of the house presents itself and can be accessed on two levels. "This was exactly the same principle as is found in a traditional Black Forest house, in which the hay cart directly accesses the attic shed from the rear of the building." However, nothing else traditional appears on the building. It is characterized by its clear forms and a technical material language of concrete, glass, and metal. The two side wings are docked to a central axis with a glass hall and entrance. The "finger" of the elevated glass library with its floating roof, which cantilevers out over the space, appears as a further development of the library Geber built for the university in Göttingen, which also takes up the motif of a finger, as does the training center in Münster. A good thirty kilometers northwest of Dortmund, at the edge of the city center, one finds the campus of the Westfälische Hochschule Recklinghausen (Recklinghausen Campus of the University of Applied Sciences) with its departments of materials technology and industrial engineering. The architectural ensemble, consisting of three main components, opened in 1999 after Gerber won the competition for the site in 1995. During a quick lunch in the university cafeteria, the dean of the faculty joins us. Even before we set off on our tour, we become engaged in an intensive discussion about the current conditions of university education—about the pluses and minuses of the European-wide Bologna reform process, the compatibility of degrees and, of course, the importance of architecture for student life at a university. Despite it being a semester break, the library is full; it is located on the upper floor of the bright, L-shaped building with the cafeteria housed on the ground floor. The forecourt resulting from the L-shape of the building is spatially "completed" to form a square by a support and two rectangular beams. Despite this openness, the overall structure gives the impression of a protected courtyard. The view seen on an aerial photograph illustrates the urban planning idea that guided the ensemble: to the right and left of a slightly sloping central axis, which follows the course of a long-existing hollow, one sees the administrative wing and the elongated frame of the building containing the lecture halls, to which the laboratories and offices, grouped around inner courtyards, are attached. A glass bridge allows students to walk from the lecture and laboratory wing into the library and cafeteria building. Pushed slightly off its

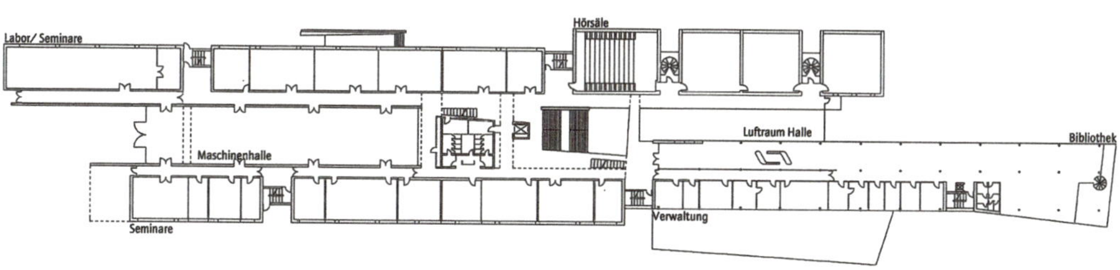

Leuphana Universität Lüneburg, Department of Automation Technology, competition first prize, 1993•1997

Leuphana Universität Lüneburg, Department of Automation Engineering, 1993•1997, floor plan, first upper storey

Westfälische Hochschule
Recklinghausen, competition
first prize, 1995•1999

axis, the building is an eye-catcher and prelude to the small ensemble. Seen from here, the lecture halls that emerge from the row of buildings appear like drawers pulled out of a dresser. They are also particularly emphasized by the wooden cladding used for the façade, which stands out from the plaster used next to it. In Recklinghausen, this produces a sensitively sculpted urban space, gently stepped and flanked by benches, trees, and hedges, a space where people like to linger. As if demonstrating this fact, a group of students who have just graduated are taking photos of themselves in robes and doctoral caps in front of the university. Inside the elongated lecture wing, visitors are welcomed by a spacious foyer with a shallow staircase running from the square to the inner foyer, which gives the space tension by dividing it into several compartments. Strižić's insistence that there be "no corridors" echoes in this hallway running through the entire building, like a reminder of Gerber's time as a student. And Gerber has indeed formulated an independent space to the sides of both auditoriums, which is divided by stairs and seats, developing a quality of its own that goes far beyond a corridor's bare function of connecting spaces.

As with the university building in Lüneburg, Recklinghausen also has several elements that will remain characteristic of Gerber's (university) school buildings in the following years. One example is the integration of the buildings into the respective landscape: the use of the topography to embed auditoriums, as with Institute of Chemistry or the auditorium center of the Justus-Liebig-Universität in Gießen. This goes hand in hand with a close dovetailing of interior and exterior space and an extraordinary landscape design for the courtyards, which can also be experienced from the outside through high glass fronts and transverse bridges. Again and again, what stands out is the exciting composition of the individual elements, which can be read as creative, abstract compositions despite their clear functionality. As with the Westfälische Hochschule Recklinghausen, this can be done along an avenue or, as in the case of the Hochschule für angewandte Wissenschaften (Würzburg-Schweinfurt University of Applied Sciences, from 2008 to 2012), by grouping the components around an open courtyard. The result is a campus that creates a sense of community and is open at two corners where representative staircases create a link to its surroundings. Exposed concrete, slender, high concrete pillars, cantilevered flying roofs, broad glass surfaces, and a constricted ground floor play just as lightly with motifs from the 1950s as does the elegant citation of Alva Aalto in the staircase, even while remaining firmly rooted in the present.

Inside, Gerber's university and laboratory buildings are characterized by a passion for staircases, which meaningfully and effectively connect the floors even as they appear to reach up into the sky, as well as for foyers generously creating additional high-quality space. This is evident not only in the buildings that Gerber has built from scratch but also in his works connecting old and new, such as the Institute for Molecular Infection Biology and the Rudolf Virchow Institute at the Universität Würzburg, which was supervised by Michael Halbeisen (who also supervised all of Gerber's laboratory and institute buildings). The building layers dovetail harmoniously to create an additional foyer: "Such a space is not a requirement in any competition, and one must stubbornly fight for it to be realized," Gerber explains his aims. "But once the space has been created, everyone loves it, because it offers something extra that no one had previously thought of." This additional quality of a building, which is what gives it an identity and creates a *Baukultur,* can also be expressed in the qualities of the materials that are used. For example, in the unusual metal cladding of the library of the Otto Stern Center (2009–2011) at the Goethe-Universität in Frankfurt am Main. The rational composition of many of his buildings from basic geometric or stereometric forms, or their functional structure, goes hand in hand with a poetic note that is reflected in details, such as the embedding of the buildings in the landscape that characterizes the comparatively strict composition of the county hall in Vechta. In that building, the frame is formed by three building wings with a pent roof that are higher up toward the city and constructed in robust red brick, and that drop down to the park-like courtyard by one storey, enclosing the central council rotunda with a light plaster façade that is itself embedded within a diagonal path and water grid. Space and material, geometry and texture, thus come together to produce an overall impression full of excitement. The competition was originally advertised for the county hall and town hall of Vechta. "Unfortunately, this concept could not be realized at this location because of landscape protection," Gerber recalls. "So another plot of land was found on which only the county hall was to be built. After the planning of the preliminary design had been completed, new legislation designated this property as a protected biotope, meaning it, too, was no longer available for construction. This prompted the desperate county administrator, Clemens-August Krapp, to hold a new competition, in which he said we could again participate. Since we had already signed a contract, this wasn't something to which I wanted to agree, or to which I would agree only if the services commissioned but not yet performed were

Westfälische Hochschule
Recklinghausen, 1995•1999

Hochschule für angewandte Wissenschaften Würzburg-Schweinfurt, competition first prize, 2004•2012

Hochschule für angewandte Wissenschaften Würzburg-Schweinfurt, 2004•2012, competition model

Hochschule für angewandte Wissenschaften Würzburg-Schweinfurt, 2004•2012

Vechta county hall, competition first prize 1985, 1997, with Horst Linn's sculpture *Landschaftstor*

Vechta county hall, competition first prize 1985, 1997

Vechta county hall, county council chamber

compensated. This created a difficult situation. I suggested that we carry out an internal competition. Our office would provide him with three different design concepts for his county hall for the new piece of land, and he could then convene a jury that would select the best of these three designs. County Administrator Krapp agreed to this proposal, appointing Jörg Friedrich as the jury chairman. The concept chosen by the county was then in fact built."

Book Paths

The move from Meschede to Dortmund proved to be a decisive step for Gerber's office, allowing it to tackle a wider range of tasks, position itself supra regionally, and occasionally focus on work abroad, such as in Saudi Arabia and even China (Gerber has yet to complete a project in China, but he currently has six skyscrapers under construction). Marius Ryrko supervises the Chinese projects from the Dortmund office, but also from Gerber's new Shanghai office, where he is supported by Benyang Gong, an expert on China. In view of this expansion, it was only logical to open further branches in addition to the new Dortmund head office; Gerber now also has offices in Hamburg and Berlin, among other places. Previously, Gerber had already opened a second location in Braunschweig, where he was able to recruit Jürgen Friedemann and Gerhard Tjarks as employees. Both men had previously worked as assistants of Meinhard von Gerkan, who had taken over the professorship of his old teacher Friedrich Wilhelm Kraemer in Braunschweig. In rapid succession, competitions were held in the following years and many were won, such as for the employment offices in Dortmund and Leipzig, for the Heinz-Bach-Haus belonging to the insurance company Continentale Versicherung in Dortmund or for the Chemical Institute in Oldenburg, which, in contrast to the Heinz-Bach-Haus, was not realized. The design for the Heinz-Bach-Haus, like others, was created in collaboration with Jürgen Friedemann, "who worked together with me in carrying out his design work in a highly structured, functional, and creative way." The building, completed in 1987, contains one hundred rental apartments as an investment of the insurance group as well as a training center for Continentale's employees. "Because of the noise produced by the nearby highway, we almost completely closed off the southern façade and situated the training center in this fourth part of the large square. Here, the building opens toward the noisy area only on the ground floor with the foyer and is otherwise oriented toward the green courtyard." The plan was for the project to be approved in accordance with Section 34 of the Building Code, which states that "a project is permissible if fits in with the properties of the surrounding area in terms of the nature and extent of its architectural use, its construction method, and the area of land to be built over, and if the development is ensured." This had been previously decided by the City Council of Dortmund. But during the planning period Gerber received a call from the city administration. The head of the City Planning Council wanted to visit him in his office at short notice. "I was curious about why he wanted to come and see me. He wanted

Twin tower, central business area, Jinan, China, 2017•2020

Presentation of certificate by Professor Hongyuan Mei to Eckhard Gerber, HIT guest professorship, Harbin Institute of Technology

to inform me that unfortunately this project could not be approved according to Section 34 and that the building authorities intended to draw up a development plan for it. This would have meant postponing the project by one or two years." Gerber spent two days brooding on the possible reason for this sudden shift of opinion, which was throwing a wrench into the planning work then underway. "Evidently, another architect in Dortmund was privately building a project of similar size, with 150 apartments, in the city center. At the time, he had very good political contacts in Dortmund, but his planning was about half a year behind ours. He wanted his project to be completed before the Heinz-Bach-Haus, since otherwise there was a risk that the housing market in Dortmund, which was already saturated, might become a problem for him." I presented this idea to the head of the insurance company at the time, Dr. Bach, who immediately realized what was going on and picked up the phone as I was standing there to call the parliamentary leader of the SPD, the Social Democratic Party. Bach told the SPD politician that if Bach had't heard by afternoon of that same day that the plan to draw up a development plan had been dropped, everything would be in the newspaper the next morning. That afternoon, the call came with the news that no development plan would be drawn up after all, so that we could carry out our project according to the original schedule and all apartments were rented before the project was completed."

At the beginning of the 1980s, Gerber also participated in international competitions, such as the Bastille Opera in Paris, for which he developed a design with Marita Langen in 1983. "It was clear to me that we wouldn't win the competition; more than eight hundred designs were submitted. But Langen took me to Paris twice, and my visits there were lovely." During this heyday of European postmodernism, the office also took part in the international competition for the Parc de la Villette in Paris, developing a design in collaboration with landscape architect Georg Penker. "The result of this competition, in which the first prize went to Bernard Tschumi, was a key experience for me and a signal for the changing zeitgeist in the planning of landscape design. Afterwards, it again became possible to work with geometric forms, axes, and symmetries—which was something that had previously not been possible because the basic approach of an English garden had almost exclusively dominated. For Georg Penker, this was probably a great disappointment. For me, however, it was more of a liberation and an opening for new approaches in landscape and open space planning." Together with Marita Langen, Gerber subsequently worked on the competition for the Haus der

Geschichte (House of History) in Bonn in 1986, for which 166 designs were submitted. "We received the second prize, but no first prize was awarded. So we won the competition, but only with a second prize. The jury was unable to reach an agreement and recommended that the six prizewinners be asked to rework their designs. Unfortunately, this is not what happened. Rather, the office of Rüdiger, in Braunschweig, which had won the third prize, was commissioned directly with the further planning. I found this decision unacceptable in view of the jury's recommendations and complained to Helmut Kohl in a letter, telling him that it was precisely in the competition for the Haus der Geschichte, which was to represent the democratic development of our Federal Republic, that it was necessary to conduct such a procedure democratically and in accordance with the jury's recommendations. Helmut Kohl passed this letter on to the Minister of Construction at the time, Oscar Schneider, since the project fell within his jurisdiction. But Schneider was the very person who had made the decision to award the commission to the third-place winner. And that's when we ended up going in circles! We achieved nothing at all and were not able to pursue the issue further." The subsequent building boom that came with the Sturm-and-Drang period of a newly reunified Germany also saw the realization of the Staats- und Universitätsbibliothek in Göttingen, the competition for which Gerber had already won in 1985 and on which Jürgen Friedemann and Gerhard Tjarks had collaborated: "I've always been interested in the construction task of libraries. However, I had no experience with their complex functional relations corresponding to their very diverse areas of use." A first engagement with the topic of libraries had already led me to participate in the 1982 competition for the new building of the Deutsche Bibliothek (German Library) in Frankfurt am Main, today the Deutsche Nationalbibliothek (German National Library). This library was the West German counterpart to the Deutsche Bibliothek (German Library) in Leipzig, a city that, before 1945, had been regarded as the center of German publishing. In order to get a feel for the construction task, Gerber arranged a visit with the director at the time of the Berliner Staatsbibliothek (Berlin State Library), Ekkehart Vesper, who in the seventies had directly helped in realizing the new library building designed by the great Hans Scharoun. "I asked Mr. Vesper to give me a tour me through the library in a variety of ways. First, I wanted to slip into the role of a new book, from delivery to cataloguing to placement in a magazine or reading room. Then, I wanted to understand the path of a book that had been in the library for some time and had to be restored. After that,

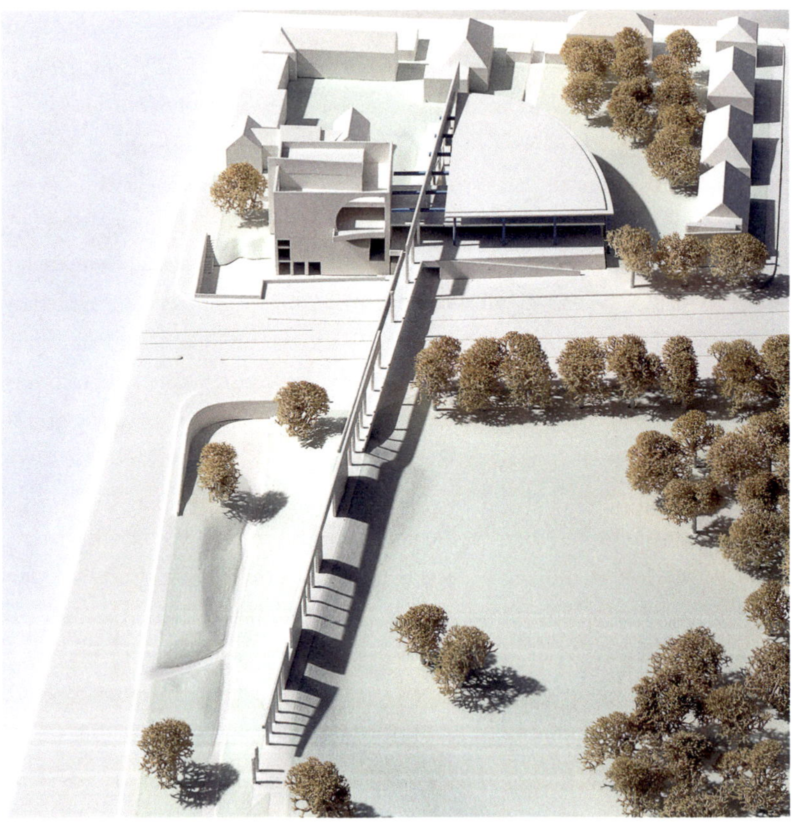

Haus der Geschichte, Bonn, competition second prize (no first prize was awarded), 1986, competition model

we followed the path of a book that is read or borrowed. And, of course, I wanted to know how I would be catalogued as a book and how my contents would be summarized in the catalogue. The last stop was to find out how I would be borrowed and delivered, as a book, by mail." Gerber then took on the role of librarian to learn more about the various stages of book processing. "I also wanted to immerse myself in the role of a library visitor and let myself be guided on the paths that they take, and in the end also in the role of a library director, in order to learn something about the overall organization and content of a library from the director's point of view. This gave me comprehensive insight into library processes, as well as an overview. I was familiar with the mail area, bookbinding, restoration, printing, and also with the reading room, the catalogue area, the checking of the books and the record-keeping. Equipped with this information, we participated in the library competition in Frankfurt and were shortlisted." The competition for the new building of the Staats- und Universitätsbibliothek in Göttingen was held three years later. The competition for the municipal museum and the Bundeskunstmuseum (Federal Art Museum) in Bonn took place at the same time. "At a colloquium for this competition, I noticed that many architects were interested in this particular project and that the same architects also wanted to work on the library in Göttingen. Since the submission of the competition for the Göttingen library was scheduled only one week later, I decided not to take part in the Bonn competition, assuming that many colleagues who had completed the Bonn competition would then no longer have time and energy for the Göttingen project." This was a strategic decision with vision. Indeed, more than 250 architects submitted entries for the museum, while only 83 architects submitted entries for the competition in Göttingen. In addition, we were able to invest all of our time in preparing our submission for the library competition. For the competition in Göttingen, Gerber was able to build on the experience he had previously gained in the project for Frankfurt. Completed in 1993, the Göttingen library is still one of the key building blocks in Gerber's oeuvre. "It was a very large project carried out by the state of Lower Saxony, and politically contested. The individual members of the state parliament preferred to organize smaller competitions for their constituencies with smaller construction projects rather than such a large project with such a huge total price at one location. Since state elections were imminent in Lower Saxony in 1986, Prime Minister Ernst Albrecht wanted to score points in the election campaign with the library in Göttingen. He asked us to build a beautiful, large model so that

Niedersächsische Staats- und Universitätsbibliothek Göttingen, competition first prize, 1985•1993

Niedersächsische Staats- und
Universitätsbibliothek Göttingen,
1985•1993, site plan competition

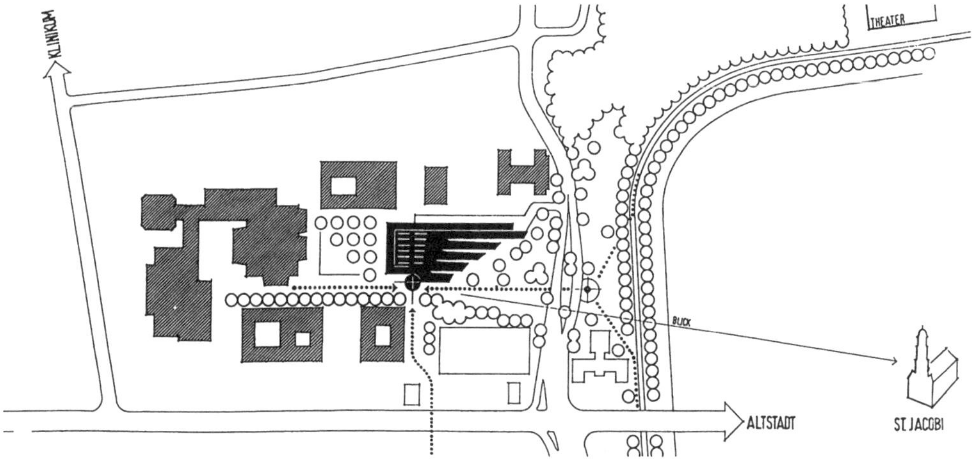

Niedersächsische Staats- und
Universitätsbibliothek Göttingen,
1985•1993, Eckhard Gerber
with the working model

we could present it accordingly." Gerber urged that construction begin as quickly as possible. He therefore proposed that the parking garage be built in the first phase of construction. "I had promised to put together what was required for the planning and tendering within six weeks. And in fact, the permits were granted in no time at all. Even without the usually required 'construction budget documentation,' we got the starting signal and, during the election campaign, we were able to lay the foundation stone with Prime Minister Ernst Albrecht in the deep excavation that had been made for the parking garage."

Here, too, Gerber proved to be an experienced strategist, as the state subsequently lacked the funds to continue the construction work. "The project would most likely not have been realized if this first construction phase had not already been cemented." For two years, nothing happened at the construction site, with the finished underground parking garage protected by a provisional sealing. Again and again, suggestions were made to redesign or downsize the project. Even the overall concept of the glass "fingers" of the library—which were intended to dovetail with the surrounding green space stretching all the way to the Old Botanical Garden—was called into question. The "finger structure" was also intended to ensure an optimal structure of functions, orientation, and organization. "Since the finger structure was the conceptual basis for our design, I stuck to it and communicated to the clients that they must have made a wrong decision in proposing that our competition design be realized. Because of the advanced planning, however, this decision could not be changed, and our copyright gave us the opportunity of sticking to this concept." Questions were also raised about the two-storey airspaces in the "fingertips." "However, these objections could also be dismissed because I was able to prove that the second floor would have to be at least one meter higher over the entire library area in order to achieve the necessary clearance, which we had compensated accordingly with the open spaces of the library. It was enough to make an appropriate note in the file and thus keep the file 'clean' for the client."

On a sunny Saturday afternoon in May, we meander through the crowded library. Are the storm clouds we see rising up on the horizon above Göttingen a distant memory of the inclemency of the time when the library was built? With the library, it's the same story as with so many construction projects: once the building has been completed and opened and is in use, the pulling and tugging that came with its construction is quickly forgotten. The light library fingers present themselves with a pleasant airiness. Our eyes

Niedersächsische Staats- und Universitätsbibliothek Göttingen, 1985•1993, opening toward the landscape

wander freely between the levels connected by stairs. This kind of freedom gives students space to think and be creative, and it is something that I myself have always appreciated in libraries. My preference probably means I am a child of Scharoun's Staatsbibliothek in Berlin—and that I am thus in good hands here in Göttingen. We stand for a long time in the high foyer framed by galleries and talk about the history of the building; we look over the bridges that cross the foyer and the floating staircase (here, again), while the steady stream of young people entering and leaving the building does not abate. Digitalization has dramatically altered the processes in the library. The huge card catalogues are no longer necessary but have been replaced by computer workstations, which was something already accounted for in the future planning. Yet the medium of the book has by no means become superfluous. And so the white metal shelves line up between the slender concrete columns, readers pile up stacks of books in their studios, students sit deep in their chairs while reading or let their eyes and thoughts wander for a moment. They look through the wide glass surfaces out onto the campus of the university and at the wonderful park-like green space designed by Hinnerk Wehberg from Hamburg, the sculptor and poet among German landscape designers. Later, when we look at the "fingers of knowledge" from the outside, the blue sky and architecture are reflected in the elongated water basin that follows one side of the library and thus contributes to the harmonious overall impression of the site. "Precisely the finger structure, so controversial during the construction, has been featured in many international publications," Gerber explains as we walk around the building. "It was featured in *Neufert* as an exceptional basic concept in library construction." The fact that the Göttingen library has found its way into the literature had particular ramifications for Gerber. "The library in Göttingen could also be seen in a French book about the most beautiful libraries in the world, which was available to the planning authority in Riyadh when it wanted to rebuild its National Library. We were invited to take part in the international competition based on this publication." The plan was to build a representative new library in Riyadh. The winner of the 1999/2000 international architectural competition was Mario Botta from Ticino, who had planned the library in Dortmund. But Botta's design wasn't built. Instead, two years later Gerber again received an inquiry from Saudi Arabia regarding whether he would be available for another competition for the National Library. "It turned out that the plan for a new building had proven to be too large and too costly. It was therefore decided to expand the existing library in the city center instead of building a new library." While Botta declined to participate in the new competition, Gerber submitted an entry. This was the foundation for the first international refocusing of his office: "We were extremely fortunate to win this competition and get the planning commission." Gerber, who immersed himself intensively in the culture and mentality of Arabia for the design, proposed to build a cube-shaped new building over the old library and to encase all of it with a sail façade on all sides. The entire new library was hoisted above the old library building with eight columns. It was a suspended construction, a complete supporting structure with a lot of steel. Design for the project continued along these lines until steel prices suddenly rose and the client demanded that we develop a new, simpler design. The project would have died otherwise. The old building was no longer to become a cultural center but was to remain part of the library. "I was shaken, and it took me days to pull myself back together. So we had to come up with a new concept, and we got to work. The new building was erected on the ground and no longer suspended, and now it took the shape of a flat square surrounding the old building, which became the book magazine. The administrative areas were located in the surrounding new building and the reading room on the roof of the old building, level with the uppermost floor." In this way, it was possible to respectfully preserve the old building and transform it into a book repository and "center of knowledge." The new King Fahad National Library building, which opened in 2015, is now considered one of the most important cultural buildings in the Kingdom of Saudi Arabia. The filigree textile façade of individual stretched white sails, which were part of the preliminary design, appears like a garment; the sails join together to form a highly recognizable, repetitive, abstract pattern, providing shade while also allowing light to pass through. The look of the original design was thus preserved. In the National Library, traditional building forms and ornaments merge effortlessly with innovative architecture to form a bright modernity. The construction of the National Library in Riyadh—which was supervised for three years by Thomas Lücking, who since then has also been in charge of all activities of Gerber Architekten in the Middle East—provided the impetus for several successful competitions in Saudi Arabia. Among these was a special design by Gerber, developed with Hannes Beinhoff: the Noble Quran Oasis northeast of the city center of Medina, which was awarded a second prize in 2014 (a first prize was not awarded). Even if the oasis occupies a singular position in Eckhard Gerber's work to date, it nevertheless seems like a synthesis of his architecture. The underlying idea sees the build-

King Fahad National Library
Riyadh, Saudi Arabia,
first competition 2002, site
plan with elevation

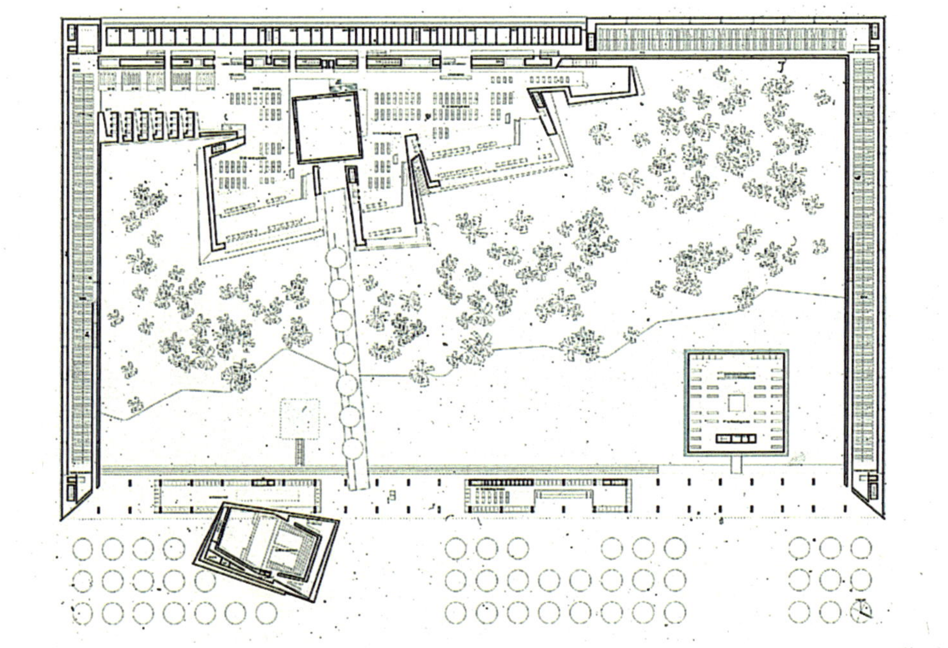

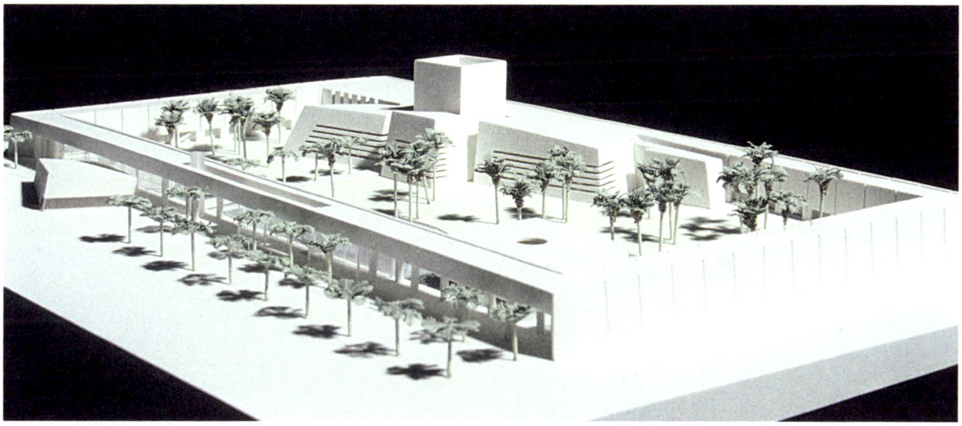

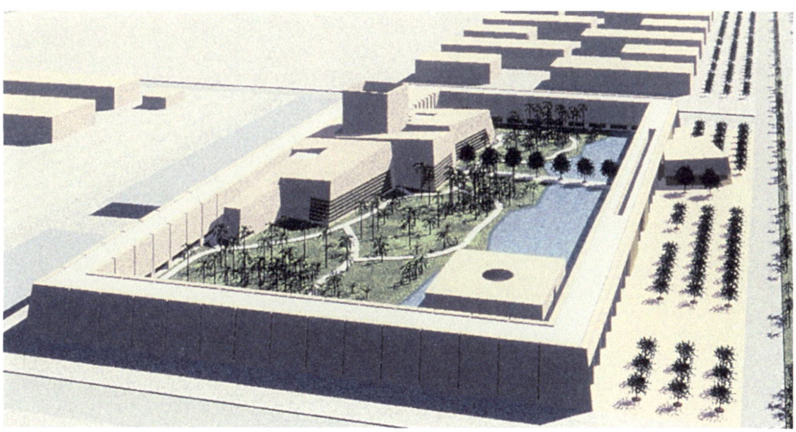

King Fahad National Library
Riyadh, first competition 2002,
competition models

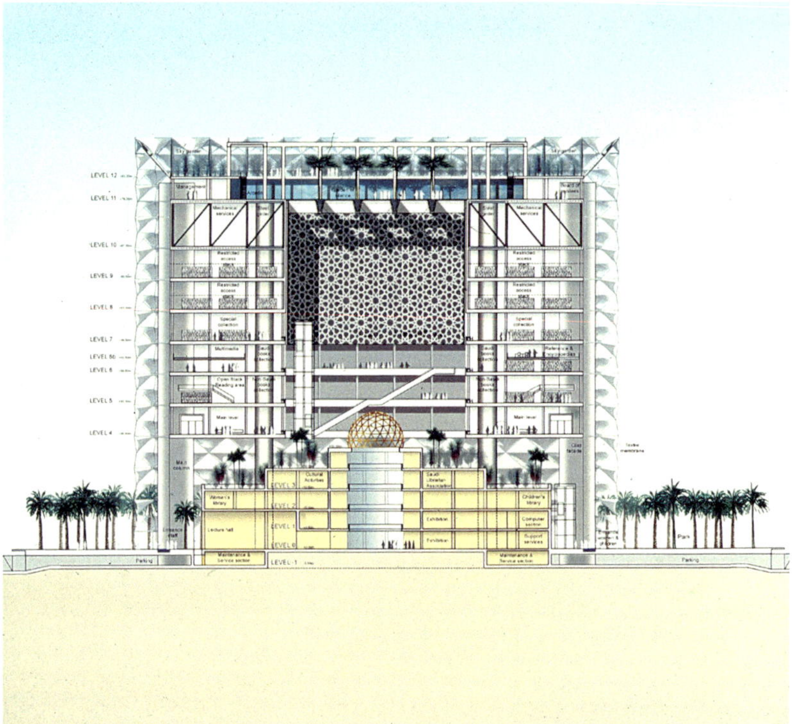

King Fahad National Library
Riyadh, Saudi Arabia, second competition, first prize, cross section, competition models

ing, with its golden roof, as a mountain “rent by the revelatory power of the Quran, receiving a distinct crack,” to cite the project description. What is characteristic for Gerber’s work is the derivation of the figure from the geometric shapes of triangle, circle, and polygon: “The circle in the center symbolizes peace and balance, the polygonal, three-dimensional roof structure looks like an ornament and engenders identity. This is the area where the museum is located, which rests on five supporting pillars symbolizing the five pillars of Islam.” Set deep in the ground, the design evokes memories of Helmut Striffler’s Versöhnungskirche in Dachau, which helped shape Gerber’s understanding of architecture so early on with such long-lasting effect, despite such a different theme and material. This is complemented by the motif of the landscape—here, in an extreme focusing of an oasis, evident even in the selection of plants described in the Quran, Sunna, and Hadith, and in the knowledge the design displays of the historical and cultural significance of Islamic gardens.

King Fahad National Library
Riyadh, Saudi Arabia,
second competition, revision

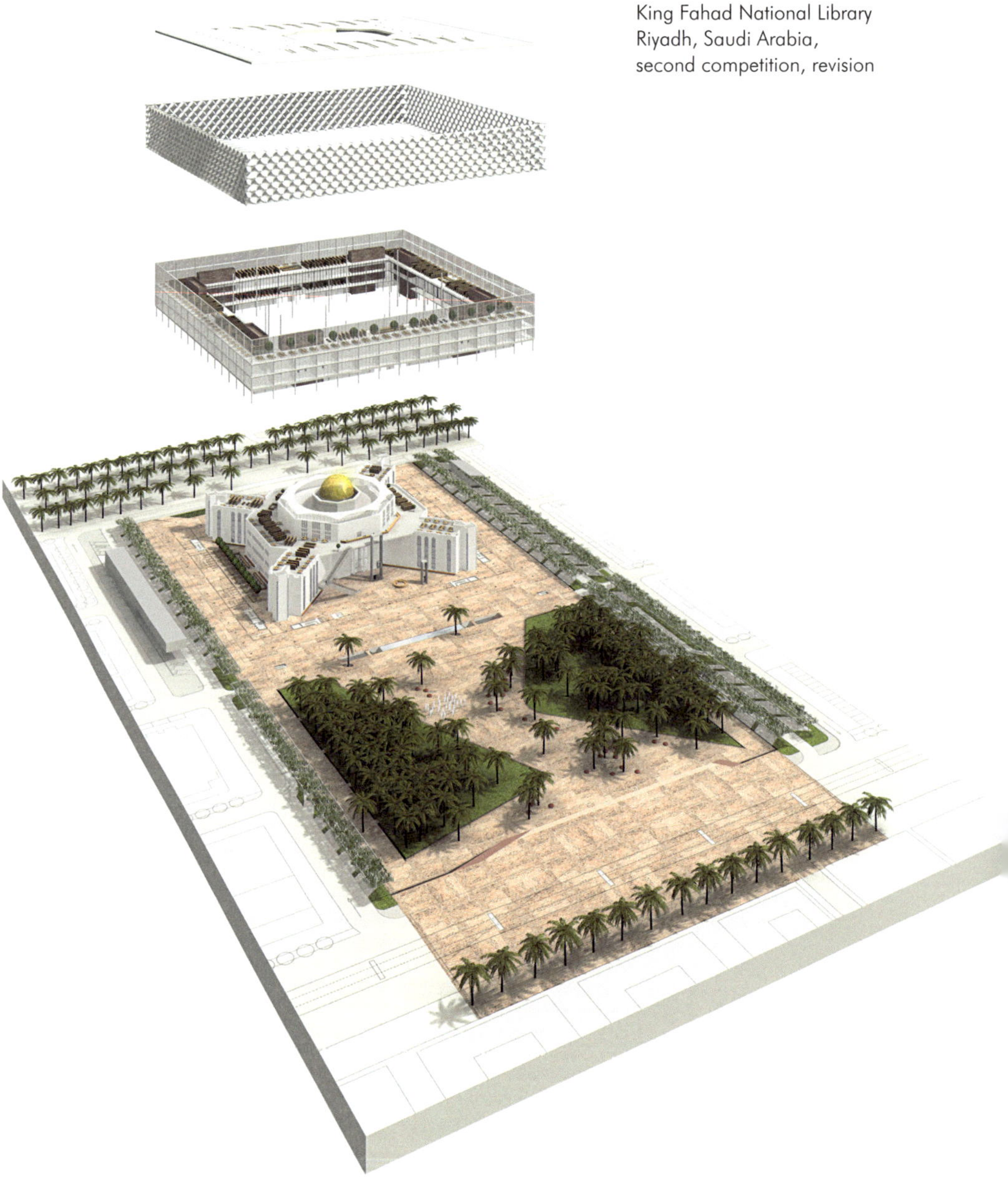

King Fahad National Library
Riyadh, Saudi Arabia, 2014,
the finished building

Entry hall

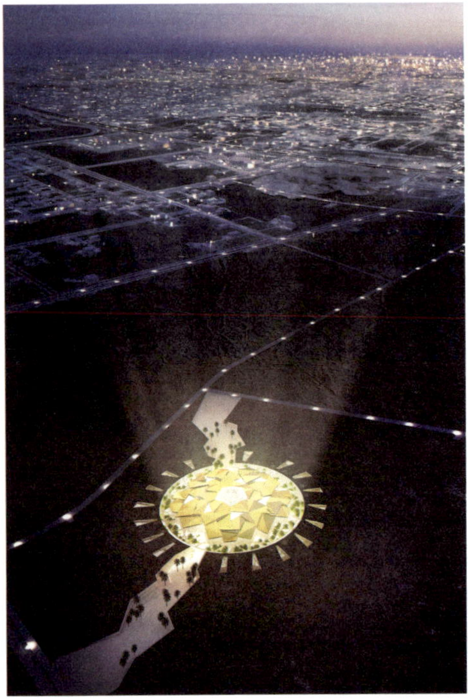

The Nobel Quran Oasis (Koran Museum), Medina, Saudi Arabia, competition second prize, 2014 (no commission has been awarded yet)

Pearl Necklaces

Anyone who sees the designed environment with open eyes quickly senses that good architecture is more than just an enclosed space. Good architecture has its roots in the spirit of its time, tasks, and ideas, while also transporting these into the future. Form may follow function, as Louis Sullivan once said. But architecture has much more to offer. It reflects all of the ways in which its architect has been shaped by culture, as well as the community in which he or she lives. And anyone who has realized several hundred buildings over a long professional life as an architect will keep designing some that turn out to be a bit more significant than the others, whether because of the special construction task, the specific conditions on site or with the client, or other favorable conditions (which are sometimes difficult to grasp). In Eckhard Gerber's work, these special buildings certainly include the Harenberg high-rise and the libraries in Göttingen and Riyadh, however different they may be; the poetically conceived music school in Leipzig; MDR's Landesfunkhaus in Magdeburg; and the Neue Messe in Karlsruhe. All of these were the result of successful competition entries that Gerber developed in collaboration with René Koblank. Trade fair buildings, in particular, which are becoming increasingly important nationally and internationally, are usually impressive simply because of their sheer size. In Karlsruhe, Gerber manages to give functionality and aesthetics a form that is equally memorable and robust, and that meets the high daily demands of constant trade fair use. Structure, wayfinding systems, and variability of use are indispensable and and must be coupled, for users, with intuitive possibilities for orientation and an atmospheric quality. Taking a bird's-eye view of the Neue Messe in Karlsruhe, one might be reminded of the geometric plan underlying a city—an especially meaningful accent in Karlsruhe, a city built according to the Enlightenment plans of Friedrich Weinbrenner. The four wings of the exhibition halls, located beneath wide roofs shimmering like silver, are situated around a green center. Glass slits cut across the roof surfaces, structuring them into compartments and at the same time clearly marking the entrances to the halls, which makes orientation easier. Cutting across from these wings, the large entrance building stands with a cantilevered roof over the approach that strikingly greets visitors—at once a welcoming gesture and a trademark. Upon entering the building, visitors are led to the foyer. This is a steel-glass construction under a floating roof, with an impressive floating staircase at the back leading up to the restaurant, conference rooms, and administration. From this bright space, the path leads to the individual

King Salman Science Oasis
(KSSO), Riyadh, Saudi Arabia,
competition first prize, 2004,
2010•2019

King Salman Science Oasis (KSSO), Riyadh, Saudi Arabia, competition first prize 2004, 2010•2019, groundbreaking with King Salman, at that time Prince Salman, (*center*) and Eckhard Gerber (*far right*)

Olaya Metro Transfer Station, Riyadh, Saudi Arabia, competition first prize, 2014

New Olaya Metro Transfer Station, realization project 2014•2019

Eckhard Gerber at a reception held by King Abdullah bin Abdul Aziz-al-Saud with German Chancellor Angela Merkel

exhibition halls, which branch off like four large wings from the central circular path surrounding the center. Everything remains in dialogue, inside and out. Navigation becomes intuitive for visitors and a system is created that could, in principle, be replicated many times over without losing any of its evident functionality, if not for the limits set by the site's dimensions. One of the halls, just to the right of the entrance, falls slightly out of this grid and is larger. Covered by a wide wooden roof construction, like the other three halls but with a visible beam construction, it serves as the center's multifunctional hall. It can be flexibly used, with variable seating to accommodate a wide variety of events, from trade shows to concerts. One particular pearl among Gerber's key works would easily fit within a quite unique collection of buildings from different stages of modernism: the Landesfunkhaus, or state broadcasting building, in Magdeburg. Dominated by the double-tower

Neue Messe Karlsruhe, competition first prize, 2000•2003, halls made of a wood construction spanning freely over eighty meters

façade of the earliest Gothic cathedral in Germany, today's capital of Saxony-Anhalt is the drama queen of German cities. It was almost completely destroyed twice, in the Thirty Years' War and in the Second World War. Yet both wars are historically far away when we visit the broadcasting center in the summer of 2017, on the island Rotehorn in the Elbe, just opposite the site of the medieval city with the cathedral dominating the cityscape. The Funkhaus, whose project manager was Jens Haake (and who has worked with Gerber Architekten for twenty-five years), is the third pearl in a string of three buildings on the island in the Elbe. The first of these was the city hall designed by Johannes Göderitz, city planning councilor in Magdeburg during the Weimar Republic and, after 1945, Gerber's university teacher at his alma mater in Braunschweig. The cubic brick building is one chief work of the Neues Bauen (New Building) movement from the 1920s in

Neue Messe Karlsruhe,
2000•2003, reception hall with
elevator and floating staircase

Neue Messe Karlsruhe,
1997, competition first prize,
2000•2003, aerial photo

Neue Messe Karlsruhe,
1997, competition first prize,
2000•2003, view into the Black Forest

Neue Messe Karlsruhe, competition first prize, 2000•2003, main entrance with wide cantilevered roof

MDR Landesfunkhaus Saxony-Anhalt, Magdeburg, with the town hall designed by Göderitz and the sculpture *Pferdetor* in the background

MDR Landesfunkhaus Saxony-Anhalt, Magdeburg, competition first prize, 1994•1998, view from the central hall to the Elbe River and cathedral

Germany and is finally slated for desperately needed renovations over the next few years. Only a few steps away stands Ulrich Müther's hypar shell of the former event center of 1969, a building protected as a historic monument—but unfortunately poorly maintained—which is now also slated for renovation. Gerber added a further accent to this world-class architectural landscape with his Landesfunkhaus, which opened in 1998. At first glance, the center appears to cut a wide circle. But the figure turns out to be a half oval opening up a magnificent view of the city of Otto the Great, crowned by its cathedral, through the completely glass façade facing the Elbe River. The city functions here as the main actor addressed by the architecture. The façade, covered with blue-violet glazed bricks, surrounds the broadcasting center like a precious cloak, playing with citations from Expressionism that range from Johannes Göderitz to Hans Poelzig. The offices of the employees of all editorial offices are located in this rear part of the building, which encompasses the central hall toward which it opens with galleries in a wide sweep. And above all of it, the roof floats on elegant steel columns, seemingly defying gravity. Here, the play of transparency and mass that we find again and again in Gerber's buildings appears to have been taken to the extreme. Indeed, it appears to have taken an entirely different turn because the cubic internal structures housing the studios, made of visible concrete, have been sensitively distributed throughout the hall. They open up to make terraces, create pathways and entrances, a built cityscape with a constant view of its counterpart, the combination of the river, the riverbank, and the cathedral. Together, they develop a common counterpoint. All of Gerber's architectural themes come together here: his signature contemporary style, developed from geometry; his combination of motifs from his design theory with a floating roof, closed wall, and free, curved form; and the uncompromising connection to the landscape, which binds the functional materialities of brick and wood, steel and glass into an overall impression that, through its interplay, creates more than its individual parts. This is an architecture that builds a bridge in finding the right design, that creates a connection and thus opens up new spaces merging with visionary sounds—toward the future, and much more.

Next pages:
Eckhard Gerber, 2017

Personal Encounters and Experiences with Architecture

Sebastian Redecke

During my studies at the TU Braunschweig in the 1980s, I managed to get one of the coveted places in the art room. It was located on the ninth floor of what was called BS4, an inconsequential new high-rise building on Mühlenpfordtstraße. Three students in the room were working on their diploma thesis at the time, and as a newcomer I was amazed at their perseverance. They sat until late into the night, working on their designs with technical pens, pencils, and T-squares and building working models. That is where I heard the name Eckhard Gerber for the first time. Two of the graduates mentioned the architectural firm, since it had been attracting attention for some time by achieving good results at competitions and was rumored to have a perfectly organized competition team. The students were assessing their chances of being able to start out as architects in the Dortmund office with exciting projects. At that time, I also noticed that the name Gerber was always among the prizewinners listed in publications. I learned that this strong commitment and its myriad successes were the basis for a rapidly growing office, which quickly included several branches and even became active worldwide. To my surprise, an assistant to one of the design professors told me that Gerber had also completed his degree in Braunschweig in the 1960s, studying at the time with Friedrich Wilhelm Kraemer and Walter Henn.

An international competition in Berlin in 1988 especially caught my interest: the Deutsches Historisches Museum (German Historical Museum) on the banks of the *Spreebogen,* the bend of the river in the center of the city. Aldo Rossi won that competition. But the fall of the Berlin Wall a year later stopped the project. Today the area is occupied by the Federal Chancellery.

Yet even in this highly important competition with 220 participants, including invitations sent to important international architects, Gerber managed to push ahead to take fifth place. I clearly remember his design: a square building to which a light bridge construction had been attached, leading to the old congress hall. None of the parts seem massive. Instead, they are mostly open and conceived to be inviting. A short time later, Gerber created his design for the high-rise Harenberg Publishing House in Dortmund. The competition was decided in 1989 and construction was already completed in 1993—with a completely different concept aligned with the situation and the task: a building of bold determination, with a look of rationality, at a location along the railway tracks. The tower was the first completed Gerber building that I visited, and I was amazed at the architectural language, which is different from that of the designs I had previously encountered. The tower with the Dortmunder U next door is unmistakable, and with every train ride through Dortmund, I see it—together with the recently built new buildings nearby—as an eye-catcher shaping the cityscape.

Eckhard Gerber and I did not get to know each other until 1994, on the campus of the Universität Göttingen. For me, the Braunschweig art room was long a thing of the past, and after my first years as an editor at *Bauwelt,* I was excited about Gerber's Niedersächsische Staats- und Universitätsbibliothek (Lower Saxony State and University Library)—a courageous architectural gesture that was a frequent topic of discussion in the city. Gerber had designed five building fingers with glass "fingertips" that aimed, through as much transparency as possible, to visually intermesh the campus via a heavily traveled road with the city center, and especially with the Jakobikirche (St. Jacobi Church) as a point of reference. The concept, communicative in the spacious and inviting building, was convincing—despite some structural savings that the client had required, including a direct pedestrian connection situated in the visual axis. But at the time I could not understand the openness, the decision to put so many glass windows on all sides of the reading room in an academic library. When it comes to concentrating and delving into books, it seemed to me, a showcase window hinders rather than helps. Why should it be a good thing to be distracted by life on campus while reading? Gerber was open to a discussion on this topic and showed me a series of different places in the building where one could read—all of them surrounded by glass, but some of them somewhat shielded. During the tour, he spoke quietly, at length, and elaborately, and he was well-informed down to the last detail about the design of his library. He struck me as modest, almost cautious. At the time, I was amazed that an architect who, to me, seemed so reserved had achieved such success and managed an office structure that had grown so quickly. A few years ago, in Riyadh, I experienced Gerber as having great tenacity while also operating with a project's goals clearly in mind and working effectively in a team.

In 1999, I met Eckhard Gerber again. A great deal of glass and an orientation toward the city center were again central themes at the MDR-Landesfunkhaus (MDR Regional Radio Broadcasting Center) in Magdeburg, Saxony-Anhalt. The building stands by itself on Rotehorn Island in the Elbe River, opposite the city center. Gerber won the competition in 1994. Once again, the decisive concept for his design was a visual relationship: the imposing backdrop of the Magdeburg Cathedral with its twin towers. Specifically, the new structure appears as a showcase window that is over seventy meters wide and occupies the entire height of the building with a view of the cathedral and its immediate surroundings. Everything is simply designed, well thought-out and without any bombastic high-tech constructions. A simple building structured like a band embraces the remaining part of the construction—a large arch that acts as a protective shell. In the central light-flooded hall, the television and radio studios, designed with a great deal of open space, have been inserted as a partially elevated "media landscape." Here, too, I remember Eckhard Gerber full of enthusiasm amid his architectural world. He explained every detail of the concept and execution to me. He was visibly satisfied, and certainly proud, to have achieved something conceptually convincing, especially with the client and a particularly demanding program, while also executing his basic idea with complete clarity, namely the local reference anchored in the cathedral. In 1986, Gerber had already won a first prize with a design centered on the theme of creating a view. His city hall on the Danube in Regensburg opened toward the opposing historical city silhouette with a wide glass front. In Regensburg, however, there was disagreement about the project—and so to this day there is no new town hall.

The extent to which Gerber's great success has become increasingly international is particularly evident in China and Saudi Arabia. In 2013, I arrived in Riyadh and accompanied Eckhard Gerber to visit what is probably one of his most interesting and convincing works: the National Library located in the city, with the unique twist that it consists of a superstructure or, more precisely, an enclosure built around the old x-shaped library from the 1970s. The outer appearance is marked by white membranes braced with a sophisticated rope system, giving them the look of sails—a feature dictated by the climate that clearly stands out in the urban environment, without aiming for an overwrought effect. Here, again, the space surrounding the building plays inwardly into the building, though this time with great subtlety. We only had two hours for the visit, but it was impressive to see how Eckhard Gerber used this time to show me and my colleagues the building in great detail and was then able to keep appointments in the city to discuss further projects and plans, all the while carrying himself with calmness and friendliness, yet also assertiveness. In the meantime, Gerber's King Salman Science Oasis—a public center intended to disseminate the technology of the future—has also been completed in Riyadh. Gerber is also planning the Olaya metro transfer station in Riyadh's city center—a courageous project on a wadi with a wide curved roof, which is to be designed as a park with palm trees echoing the desert sand dunes. Further infrastructure projects are planned in Mecca. As soon as we had said goodbye, Eckhard Gerber was already on his way to the next appointment in Jeddah. His skill and sureness are always apparent, but to me the key to his success appears to be his knowledge of human nature, which also extends to other cultures, coupled with his attentiveness and qualities as a mediator.

The Gap in the Fence

Dietrich Sattler

Two Years Spent as a Youth in the GDR: The Beginning of a Life-long Friendship

The village of Großheringen sat at the spot where the charming Ilm River flowed into the Saale, but it was a desert as far as Weimar's churches were concerned—or that's what I, as a twelve-year old boy, heard Bishop Mitzenheim from Eisenach say to my mother, a member of the parish council, as he announced the new pastor. I shuddered. And then I accompanied her to the other end of Thuringia, to Großenlupnitz near Eisenach, where I first heard your father, Eckhard, preach, though he was visibly suffering. Afterwards, in the parish garden, you and I saw each other for the first time—you had light blond hair, mine was dark black. Because you had enrolled late in school in 1945, you had missed a year, and so you came into my class. That was in the summer of 1951, if I'm not mistaken. You were a year older than I: I was 12 and you were 13.

The parsonage was closer to the school, up the village road, and everyone heard me shouting "Eckhard!" on workday mornings. But our hillside garden behind the courtyard, laid out toward the Ilm, bordered the parish garden, and a gap that we soon made in the fence shortened the path between us. We agreed on everything—and of course also in our rejection of the inhuman political regime. It was only in chess that we each played our own game. When the seventh and eighth-grade classes gathered in the schoolyard to sing the Socialist marching song, "You have a goal before your eyes / to make your way in this world," we sang instead, "You have a board before your eyes"—a joke that was also a play on the old farmers' saying, "To have a board in front of your face," meaning to have been made docile and dumb. That was our succinct reply to those ideological impositions. And even though the name "Peace Race" was propagandistic, we followed this contest on the radio and were thrilled when the cycling idol Täve Schur once again broke away from the peloton, riding alone to a stage victory. And there's one thing about this story that must be mentioned—it's small but by no means insignificant. Your bicycle had a stem handlebar, signaling your stylistic determination, that your eldest brother Eberhard had smuggled from across the border, where he attended a Western boarding school.

And here I should also mention your first construction project, in which I was also involved. It happened during a holiday stay with the class teacher and school principal Herbeli Hensel on the Baltic Sea: a dual sand castle for boys and girls adorned with the Rudelsburg and Saaleck castles, which we made out of clay from a pit we had found on the roadside. The building won first prize in a sand castle competition—with a Hanseatic cog for a trophy that can still be seen in the school in Großheringen. The following summer, when the expropriation of our farm was treacherously announced, we fled like thousands of other farmers via Berlin to the "free West." It was to your credit, Eckhard, that we found each other a few years later.

Ad multos annos

Speech by Kaspar Kraemer
Edited by Dieter Nellen

Saturday, November 12, 2016: around 500 guests, including representatives from politics, public administration, architecture, and planning, have gathered together in the Cathedral, as it is called, beneath the light dome of the Dortmunder U, a cultural center located in the first high-rise built in Dortmund, in 1926/27. Eckhard Gerber has transformed the historic city landmark, as a flagship project for the European Capital of Culture Ruhr 2010, into a multithematic venue for art and creativity. The speech celebrating the project (which is documented here in excerpts) will be given by Gerber's long-time friend Kaspar Kraemer, owner of the eponymous office Kaspar Kraemer Architekten BDA in Cologne and son of the architect and teacher at the Technischen Universität Braunschweig (Technical University of Braunschweig), Professor Dr. Ing. Friedrich Wilhelm Kraemer (1907–1990):

"Friendship and a Binding Foundation of Values"

It is our task to remember and appreciate fifty years—half a century—of successful architectural work. Fifty years of a life's journey that you began on October 13, 1938, in a small community in Thuringia, riding on a "wave of dreams" that washed you here to North Rhine-Westphalia. A life's journey with ups and downs and many stations, but which in retrospect appears to have resolutely followed a straight line.

We are bound together by a long and collegial friendship, something which doesn't happen so often among architects but has resulted here from a kindred basic disposition and a foundation of similar values.

Analysis of a Success Story

This is why I am now standing here, presenting some thoughts that I consider to be essential—for your work, and thus for the work of Gerber Architekten. I even want to go so far as to attempt an analysis of your success—to uncover its secret methods. It will become clear that this success is not coincidental but justified—that the steady demand for your office's work is not a result of caprice, luck, or connections but must be seen as the result of intellectual calculation, rationality, and the power of your thinking. I would like to show that your life's work is the result of a conception—an intellectual attitude that supports your work: a design philosophy that has made you and your staff one of the great, consistently successful German architectural firms for more than half a century. Today, this is a firm with 175 employees in Dortmund, Hamburg, and Berlin as well as branch offices in Riyadh and Shanghai, that realizes projects for every setting, magnitude, and challenge.

Personality and Experiences at the University

Two moments seem to me to be crucially responsible for this success, and I would like to briefly touch on both of them before I try to bring them together in the architecture you have created. These moments are, first, your personality, as shaped by your background and parental home, and second, the experiences you gained while studying at the university, which can be summed up with the term "the Braunschweig school." To me, it is the connection or even the fusion of these two essential elements that clearly explains your success.

A German Pastor's House

As the third child of six brothers and sisters in Thuringia, you were born into the house of a German pastor and thus into the institution that, since Luther, has for centuries shaped German spiritual, family, and intellectual life like no other. The village community in which you grew up was small and manageable, yet marked by hierarchy. Your primary school class encompassed four years, meaning four classes were taught in one room. Hence, if you wanted to, it was possible to learn a lot from the other students—and you wanted to learn a lot.

A Young Architect Influenced by the Church

The situation of post-war scarcity in your village also awakened your skills as a craftsman early on and allowed you to mature into an experienced builder at an early age. At first, you built structures for all kinds of animals—the whole food chain, as it were, from rabbits to chickens. Later, you built gazebos that you probably managed to ennoble as little pavilions. At an early age, you thus experienced the joy in craftsmanship—in making, manufacturing, designing, and implementing—that has never left you.

Two Worlds: Conviction and Necessity

This world has deeply shaped you, dear Eckhard, and it also took place within sight of the Wartburg—symbolically speaking, under the eyes of the Reformer Luther himself. And so, it is no wonder that you sometimes display a pastoral habitus to this day. Especially when you dress—as you usually do—in a white shirt and a black suit.

This was a special, extraordinary world, even more so because after 1945, this world was merely tolerated, later becoming something that those in power actively fought against and wanted to do away with. That was an essential threat to you and your family. For an adolescent, it must have also been a heavy feeling: having to live in an environment that constantly forced you to outwardly conceal your parents' opposition to the political system, to move in two worlds while being compelled to satisfy both—the one out of conviction, and the other out of necessity.

It is typical for you that you made a virtue out of this conflict, since this weighing of words, this ambiguity, this double existence was a training that later served you as a designer. You were able to view it as an intellectual challenge—formulating essays, for instance, that allowed one side to feel represented while the other could not object. This oscillation between criticism and affirmation has created a kind of mental alertness within you that has been, and remains, enormously helpful for analyzing architectural problems and tasks—especially in competitions: for the challenge in design, too, is reconciling different parameters with each other and coming to an orderly form through endless experimentation.

A Youth Spent near Weimar

You graduated from high school in Apolda near Weimar—while also performing in a jazz band that you helped found, and that you directed and supported with your musicality, playing trumpet, flute, and piano. Here, too, you knew how to use and master various instruments. As so often in biographies, you had an admired and revered teacher and mentor. He taught you art, German, and mathematics, and you helped him develop posters and display boards. He taught you the basics of graphics and design, and you discovered your talent in drawing. Often, you headed outdoors to hike and explore, and it was in the hills and wide fields around Weimar that you developed your sense for references to the landscape that is responsible for the masterful way you so often set your projects in their surroundings.

From One Germany to the Other: Berlin—TH Braunschweig

As a pastor's son you were not allowed to study in the GDR, and so all that was left for you was the prospect of a subordinate job or escape, which you carried out in 1957, and which you experienced as a deep moment of freedom. You completed a further year of high school in West Berlin, which was required beyond your East German education, and began your studies at the Technische Hochschule Braunschweig in 1959, driven by a desire to learn and a will to develop yourself. You wanted to do something, build something (up), to be free and active, independent and successful.

At the time, the TH Braunschweig was ruled by a "triumvirate" of professors—Friedrich Wilhelm Kraemer, Walter Henn, and Dieter Oesterlen. Three great teachers who laid the foundation for the architectural education that has come to be so widely recognized as the Braunschweig school, and whose principles are condensed in your work, dear Eckhard, as if focused by a lens. Which brings me to the second formative moment of your developmental path: your studies in Braunschweig.

Gerber Architekten: Competition as a Brand

Today, the brand "Gerber Architekten" is a synonym for architects who focus on competitions. There are but a few firms that base their success almost exclusively, and over so many years, on the results of competitions. A total of 1500 entries demonstrate the impressive scope of your work, including 200 first prizes! Just what this means can only be understood by someone who has had to prove what they can do in competitions themselves. The countless hours of struggling for the good, decisive idea; the effort of finding it and working it out; the search to express it most succinctly, in a convincing, attractive form; the nights spent working, the refining of plans, explanatory reports, and models; the joy of finishing a project followed by the hoping and waiting for the evening call from the jury; the elation of one outcome, the disappointment of another—this emotional roller coaster is an almost unbearable mixture of widely different feelings, of inspiring enthusiasm and sobering disappointment. That's what the word "competition" means.

And now multiply all of that by 1500 submissions, with 6.5 defeats for every win. How much stamina, how much strength, how much energy, mental and physical toughness, must one have to achieve this? And not only for ten years, which is how long most firms are able to keep up this pace—but for half a century, from the beginning to the present day. Incredible, amazing, magnificent! How can something like this succeed? There must be a system behind it, because the power of this achievement cannot be a coincidence.

Attitude as a System

On the contrary: this power is related to a fundamental concept, an attitude of life, work, and spirit based on principles and values like those modeled and taught in Braunschweig—ideas that are still valid today and, in my opinion, remain the constituents of good architecture. It is their application that distinguishes architecture, or "creative building," from "mere building" and that are responsible for elevating a building into the realm of architecture, rather than remaining among the indistinguishable mass of everyday buildings—in other words, for whether a building moves us, or even inspires us, or whether it leaves us indifferent, disgruntled, angry, or in the worst case, furious.

The Basic Law and Teaching Principles of the Braunschweig School

The Braunschweig school has formulated a clear answer to the question of what turns a building into a work of architecture, or—to put it pointedly—what turns a building into an image of pleasure, joy, or even beauty: it is its fundamental relationship to order. This is the Basic Law of the Braunschweig doctrine.

Architecture worthy of the name can only develop from the clever, or thoughtfully articulated, formulation of suitable construction and logically structured layout, and from their combination in a pleasing image. Drawing is therefore less a brilliant kind of sketching than a way of thinking and reflecting on paper, and designing is thus a spiritual-intellectual process that makes the highest of demands.

We all know that construction and function are subject to certain rules of statics, meaningfulness, and logical assignment that can be learned, appropriated, and communicated. *Firmitas* (Latin for strength) and *utilitas* (Latin for usefulness) can be determined, "correct" and "incorrect" can be assessed according to natural laws and logic. In the third area, embodied in *venustas* (beauty), this is much more difficult.

But it was the promise of the Braunschweig school to regard these aesthetic rules, the rules of *venustas,* as teachable; to believe that a human being could train their aesthetic judgment and discover the foundations of beauty, and that beauty could be traced back to rules of proportion, scale, relation—i.e., of order.

This was a convincing, even inspiring thought, which was taught and articulated in particular by my father, Friedrich Wilhelm Kraemer.

Legibility and Proportionate Design

The legibility of form in its cubic appearance, in its plasticity and sculptural power, became a basic law of the aesthetic appearance of a building, and the compositionally correct setting of its volumes was the essential prerequisite for successfully arranging space, form, and architecture.

Legibility of form and proportionate design of the surfaces that enveloped it and shaped it, the right setting of its volumes: is this not what radiates toward us in all of Eckhard Gerber's works? And are the best buildings not those that develop their effectiveness from the simplicity of their basic composition, their clearly defined positioning in the urban space and landscape, and the proportionate, harmonious design of their surfaces, as well as the choice of colors and materials?

And is it not these few constituents—which also shape the beauty of form and appearance in all buildings—that delight us? And is it not these few, fundamental moments that pleasantly distinguish buildings designed by Gerber Architekten from so many others?

Order and Beauty in/of Architecture

The application of the principles of the Braunschweig school in almost all of the buildings designed by Gerber Architekten manifests an attitude that convincingly assembles the most difficult, functional, and constructive of contexts into clearly legible large-scale forms, and that transforms these forms into a spatial composition enlivened by the finesse of its details and the disciplined application of color and material.

The work of Gerber Architekten manifests an attitude that has lost none of its relevance even today. On the contrary: our built environment would look better if we were to more deeply reflect on this attitude. After all, it's true: it is necessary to create order in a confusing, pluralistic world—order in purpose, construction, and form. The fact that this order is the foundation of beauty, and that there is a longing for it deeply rooted in people—these are reliable aspects on which one can build. In a turbulent world, it is more necessary than ever to reflect on the power that architecture, design, and *Baukultur* in general have to establish order, create identity, and shape society. Architects and engineers, urban and landscape planners, are therefore faced with a great humanistic task. Meeting this task is the great challenge of all planning professions.

The Task of Architects

Architects face the task of ensuring that people feel comfortable in this world, that they improve the world through their actions. This longing for improvement and this aspiration is entirely alive in you, dear Eckhard. The architect—as Karl Friedrich Schinkel proudly put it—is by definition the ennobler of all human relations. This will to refine, to design, is the motor of your commitment and the basis of your strength. And it is because this longing for improvement, for shaping the world, for order according to spiritual principles, is alive in you, dear Eckhard, as the product of your childhood, your youth, and your studies, that you have achieved what we can admire today. You yourself will see it as a tremendous gift.

But even if these principles are no longer negotiated in a common public sphere, architecture still stands on the foundation I have tried to adumbrate. And we see in the work of Gerber Architekten that this foundation has lost nothing of its load-bearing capacity over the years, indeed, that it "indestructibly" and consistently carries the weight of what is great and special.

Creative Will, Courage, and Responsibility

The principles of the Braunschweig school, the teachings of those years, have deeply influenced you, dear Eckhard, and through you, your firm. In their simplicity, which might almost be called Protestant, they have continued to coalesce to the present day with the conditions of your origin, your early becoming, to form a spiritual and living cosmos. The tasks change, but your attitude remains: "It is the soul that builds itself a body" (Friedrich Schiller). This sentence will always summarize the power your work has to point beyond us, toward what makes it special and magnificent, your fifty years of a will to design, your willingness to take risks and assume responsibility, and its brilliant results.

It is the hope of all of those friends and admirers gathered here today—and especially of those of us who are both—that you and your firm, Gerber Architekten, may continue to succeed in this task and achieve, for a long while still, a "great number of extraordinary things," that you "remain firm in will." This we wish for you and those close to you, and to your employees. The privilege of being counted among those friends and admirers makes me proud and happy. Dear Eckhard, *ad multos annos*!

Dortmund: Engagement for the Cityscape and Urban Society

Gerhard Langemeyer

What makes a city like Dortmund so livable and lovable that a renowned architectural firm decides to keep its headquarters here—despite international success and offices in Riyadh and Shanghai? A local politician would say: Dortmund is a growing city that has managed to achieve structural change. Dortmund used to be a city of coal, steel, and beer. But the mines are closed, and the steel production has been relocated to Duisburg. From among Dortmund's large breweries, only one remains: the old beer brands are now being brewed under one roof. And today, Dortmund is a city of science with state-of-the-art technology in many young and old companies. The number of jobs is increasing, and there are plenty of opportunities for leisure, recreation, and culture. The emblems of these opportunities are the new PHOENIX See, the artificial lake on the site of the former steelworks in Hörde, and Dortmund's new concert hall. The share of green space in the city is well over fifty percent and the sports on offer go far beyond Borussia Dortmund, the soccer club founded in 1909.

But if you ask the locals, the answer is usually: it's the people who live here, their engagement in the city's social fabric. The architect Eckhard Gerber is one of these people. Like most people in Dortmund, he came to this city for work. He is active in the city's culture, plays the trumpet, served for many years as chairman of the Dortmunder Kunstverein (Dortmund Art Association), and sometimes invites guests to a sculpture exhibition in his garden at the Tönnishof in Dortmund-Kley.

There, you can see his architectural signature. The sensitive handling of the old building is evident in the interplay between the old manor house from

1884 and the modern extension from 1985, which was supplemented in 2003 by a conversion of the former stable building into offices—today the headquarters of Gerber Architekten.

The Stadtgarten U-Bahn station, completed in 1982 according to a design by Gerber, is anything but a typical transportation infrastructure site. It looks more like a pagoda or a garden pavilion with a lot of glass: a flat building with a fountain in a garden environment, a unique solitary complex. I won't hide the fact that I have always found it exciting. Here, we see the value of the city's decision not to work with standard models for transit stations but to use a competition to find an independent solution at each location.

At the same time, the construction of the subway offered an opportunity to correct urban planning decisions of the early postwar period and completely redefine streets and squares in the city. For example, instead of four lanes of dense traffic running north to south, we now have a spacious boulevard with four rows of trees, plenty of space for pedestrians, and the Europa Fountain.

"At the end of the war in 1945, 95 percent of the city's buildings and streets had been destroyed. At the sight of the devastated city, British officers advised leaving it as a ruin and building a new city center next to it. But Dortmund decided in way that reflected its nature. In 1945, the city planning office was already preparing for a new beginning. A development plan for the city center established a new road network. Its basic structure: Kuckelke and Kleppingstraße would form the new north-south axis, and Kampstraße and Brüderweg the new west-east axis. The width of these routes was set at thirty-two meters. For the nearby roads leading to and intersecting with these axes, this required significant changes and adaptations. The city embankment and roads running along it were to be transformed into a wide ring road around the city, keeping traffic out of the city center while enabling a ring of green space and parking for cars—a simple plan!

In order to achieve all of this, the entire inner city was declared a reallocation area in 1947, and a reorganization plan was developed by 1949. All property in the area was affected. The plan succeeded after years of proceedings and negotiations. Reallocation reduced the number of plots that existed in 1939 in the area that would late become the new city center from 1,798 to only 832; and instead of the 1,240 previous owners at the end of the war, there were now 694. The total area used for traffic and transportation was ultimately equal to that available for construction. The Hellweg remained unchanged. Here, too much had survived the war.

Urban planning as the result of a total destruction of buildings and the subsequent dissolution of the urban structures that had grown up over time, guided by transportation planning and the will to act quickly. Planners opened up the densely built-up city center and the northern section of the inner city, which had been completely built in and lacked light.[1] After the war, Dortmund could no longer shine with a unique old city center that had developed over centuries. The rebuilt medieval churches of the inner city stood amid rapidly erected buildings from the 1950s and 1960s that differed little from what could be seen in other cities. One exception was the theater, opened in 1966 and built according to a design by the architects Rosskotten and Tritthart. But even this building had to face negative assessments by contemporary architectural critics, who charged the city with failing to completely realize the building's design out of a misguided intention to save money.[2]

Urban planning responded to the overall situation with continuous improvements in concepts for the city. The formula consisted of city-planning and architectural competitions, as well as the requirement that a design advisory board participate in construction projects. Eckhard Gerber and his team at Gerber Architekten have won numerous competitions and received numerous awards. This has benefited the city of Dortmund, elevating the quality of its architecture.

Seventy-three-meters high, directly next to the railway tracks not far from the main railway station, the Harenberg City Center has embodied modern Dortmund since 1993. Twenty-three floors in a high-rise with space for up to 600 employees, located behind a building popularly called the "slice of cake," with contours following the Wallring, or embankment that surrounded the old city. A glass hall connects the shorter building to the tall northern section, structured by a clear, grid-shaped façade of concrete openings. This urban planning solution is perfect and striking. Anyone approaching the building from the main station on the Wallring can gauge its effect.

Bodo Harenberg built the building for his publishing house as well as other companies. With an ambitious cultural program in the so-called Amphisaal (Amphihall) and the glass foyer, he created a first-class venue. His personal commitment gave life to this cultural meeting point. With this building, he's done the city a great service. It is a bitter loss that, after the sale of the publishing house and the building, the new owners were not able to continue the cultural program.

In 1988, Eckhard Gerber won first prize in a competition organized by the city of Dortmund for the nursing home Am Zinsweg in the Körne city dis-

[1] Hans Magoley and Norbert Wörner, *Architekturführer Dortmund* (Dortmund: Fr. Wilh. Ruhfus, 1984), 61.

[2] Hans Schwab-Felisch, "Ein Kompromiß für viele Jahre: Das Theater Dortmund," *Theater heute*, April 1966.

trict. The building was opened in 1993. It is characterized by a fan-like basic structure that opens toward the nature around it. The design of the open spaces and surrounding landscape plays an important role in Eckhard Gerber's plans.

At the employment office, completed in 1995, on the north side of the main railway station, the angled buildings along the roadside define the urban space; a park opens at the rear. "The façade defining the street space appears austere, cubic, and closed, while the façade on the side of the park, turned toward the landscape, appears open and transparent. The light steel-glass constructions reflect the surfaces of the water in the park and the green surroundings."[3] The building supports and follows the linking routes from the main station to the cultural center Dietrich-Keuning-Haus.

The new building for the Justizzentrum (Justice Center), completed in 2000, makes a striking impression with its well-proportioned, clear, and simple forms, and it benefits from the design of the square between the old district court and the new building.

Eckhard Gerber achieved particular success with the expansion of the Dortmunder Volksbank. In 2001, he added a glass extension to an old building from the 1960s. A single roof projecting across both buildings connects old and new. An impartial observer might suspect that this had been planned from the beginning. The design incorporates the street space of Betenstraße and invites visitors to come into the hall of tellers, flooded with daylight, which is sometimes also used as a venue for events. From the hall, the view goes out through the windows toward two churches, the Marienkirche and Reinoldikirche. The architect displays transparency and a sense for how to integrate the cityscape.

After the Harenberg City Center, Eckhard Gerber made another striking contribution to the city's urban planning with a second high-rise building. In 2006, the RWE Tower, a twenty-two-storey building with a lenticular floor plan, was constructed on the Platz von Amiens. Covered with dark, polished granite, it stands out from the usual glass or concrete façades. Placed diagonally on the site, the RWE Tower occupies a space of its own—a counterpoint that clearly stands out from the surrounding buildings, creating a new city square and links between the city center and the main railway station.

For more than fifteen years, the brewery group Brau und Brunnen had been unsuccessful in finding a subsequent use for the former Union-Brauerei (Union Brewery) on Rheinische Straße, which it no longer needed. It was

[3] Horst Glaser, *Architekturführer Dortmund 1983–2000* (Hagen: Ardenku-Verlag, 1999), 66.

only when the group proposed to set down new roots by building a company headquarters and offered to donate the brewery tower, built by Emil Moog in 1927, to the city free of charge on the condition that a use for it could be found, that it was possible to develop an urban planning solution for the site. Richard Rogers had already proposed an urban planning concept that would reroute Brinkhoffstrasse and reorganize the intersection at the Wallring.

In the tower, the depth of the spaces and low levels of daylight suggested use as a museum. In the first round, I suggested that the building be renovated according to standards for trade shows and that it be used to present the holdings of the Museum am Ostwall (Museum Ostwall). I had already proposed a new building for the Museum am Ostwall when I took office as head of the city's Culture Department. I did not think that the plans to reconstruct the old museum, for which Eckhard Gerber had also submitted a design, would lead to the desired result. The museum building was the former Prussian Oberbergamt (Mining Office), built in 1875 and partly destroyed during the war. In this building, it would not have been possible to retrofit the air conditioning technology indispensable for a museum.

After the city council had in principle approved the agreement with Brau und Brunnen, an architectural competition was launched. The jury did not award a first prize but rather three second prizes. I found the concept of Gerber Architekten immediately convincing and suggested to the city council that the design be realized without any subsequent changes.

The opening up of the space toward the outer wall allows the generosity of the floor spaces to be retained. The newly created "vertical"—an open space extending across all floors—with its visitor-friendly escalator system is reminiscent of the Centre Pompidou in Paris. Visitors can glimpse the size and uniqueness of the building by looking up into the "Cathedral." The museum's collection is housed on the upper floors, where the ceilings are higher. An addition to the sixth upper storey is a room with skylights for exhibitions. Politically, the project was highly controversial. In dialogue with the state of North-Rhine Westphalia, the project was further developed into a Center for Art and Creativity that could be realized with a grant from the state as part of the Ruhr Capital of Culture 2010. Today, it is not least of all the video installations by Adolf Winkelmann that have made the Dortmunder U into a new old landmark of the city. An investor competition put out for bidding parallel to the conversion of the Dortmunder U resulted in the construction of two vocational colleges, a large underground parking garage, and an office building to the north. This choice of procedure, however, meant that the realization of the winning design by Gerber Architekten was delayed until 2014. But the simple and clearly structured building complex now makes a captivating impression with its open space concept and the choice of red fired clinker bricks, reflecting the Dortmunder U.

Baukunstarchiv NRW: Scenes of an Architectural Location with a Dual Function

Wolfgang Sonne

The Baukunstarchiv NRW, or Architectural Archive of North Rhine-Westphalia,is a new state-wide institution among Dortmund's lighthouse cultural organizations. Eckhard Gerber played a decisive role in its creation, in two respects. Specifically, the project Baukunstarchiv NRW at the eastern city ramparts, or Ostwall, in Dortmund consisted of two construction sites that were not necessarily connected but fortunately came together: the establishment of the institution Baukunstarchiv NRW and the rescue, preservation, and conversion of the former Museum am Ostwall (Ostwall Museum), in Dortmund. Eckhard Gerber has long worked to support both, and so it is only fitting that he is now able to celebrate his eightieth birthday with a symposium and an exhibition at the Baukunstarchiv NRW at the Ostwall.

Scene One: Ostwall Construction Site

The Haus am Ostwall has a long and eventful history. It was built between 1872 and 1875 by the Berlin architect Gustav Knoblauch as the Preußisches Oberbergamt (Prussian Mining Office) on the outer ring embankment. After it had become too small for the authority, which supervised the entire mining industry from the Lower Rhine to the North Sea, the Dortmund city architect Friedrich Kullrich converted it in 1911 into the Städtisches Museum für Kunst und Kulturgeschichte (Municipal Museum of Art and Cultural History). While the exterior remained unchanged, the roofed atrium inside the building, which has survived to this day, was the monumental jewel of the house. After its partial destruction during the Second World War, the building was rebuilt from 1945 to 1957 as an art museum by the municipal building department under museum director Leonie Reygers.

The removal of the remaining upper floors made it possible to create the skylight halls desirable for an art museum, while the reduced brick cladding of the façades announced a modest but solid new beginning.
From then on, the building made an international name for itself as the Museum am Ostwall—soon becoming too small for the growing demands of an internationally active museum institution. Ideas arose to expand or move the museum. As early as the 1920s, the city architect of the time, Wilhelm Delfs, had proposed building on the parcel of land shaped like a slice of cake on its narrow side facing the city. Eckhard Gerber again took up this idea in a draft in 2002, in which the aim was to utilize development at the location to preserve the house with technology fit for the future and a larger area. His design, which he prepared for the Freunde des Museums am Ostwall (Friends of the Museum Ostwall), provided for an extension to the existing building that would revive the street lines of the historical street plan, which no longer existed at this location because of the park established in the post-war period, to thus fill in the historical block with a sharply angled construction. As with Delfs's plan, the building would have received a distinctive face toward the city center in addition to the main façade on the Ostwall.
But instead of this design, which would have continued the building history of the site, things turned out differently: looking ahead to the European Capital of Culture 2010, the Museum am Ostwall moved to the historically significant building of the Dortmunder U, which is also a landmark of the city and has now been preserved through the transformation from a brewery warehouse to a cultural center. Eckhard Gerber was given the commission to design the conversion of this striking monument after winning a competition. But this left the Haus am Ostwall standing empty, its future open.

Scene Two: Archive Construction Site

The idea of an archive for architectural media based on the model of important university collections in Berlin, Munich, Karlsruhe, or Zurich became reality in Dortmund with the founding of the Archiv für Architektur und Ingenieurbaukunst NRW (Archive for Architecture and Civil Engineering NRW) at the Faculty of Architecture of the Universität Dortmund in 1995. The initiators were Uta Hassler and Norbert Nußbaum, who held the chairs of historic preservation and building history, respectively. In keeping with the *Dortmunder Modell Bauwesen,* an educational concept for architecture and urban planning developed at the Universiät Dortmund, the archive collected materials from both architectural and civil engineering in a broad

range of media, growing rapidly. In particular, the papers and materials of the retiring generation from the postwar period of German reconstruction threatened to be completely lost; they were often saved from being discarded only on very short notice.
In addition to preserving older, endangered holdings, the archive's strategy from the outset also included securing the holdings from important current architecture and engineering firms for the long term. This is how the archive came into contact with Eckhard Gerber, who helped expand the archive by donating a first, partial portfolio of material. In addition to the founders of the *Dortmunder Modell Bauwesen*—the architect Harald Deilmann and the civil engineer Stefan Polónyi (recently joined by the architect Josef Paul Kleihues)—as well as numerous architects from the postwar period, with Eckhard Gerber the archive now held materials from an important, currently active architectural firm that could continue to contribute to the archive's collections through its ongoing work. Further acquisitions of partial holdings were agreed upon after the archive found a long-term site.

Scene Three: Ostwall Construction Site

After the museum moved out, the future of the building at the Ostwall was uncertain. Although it was immensely important for the city's history, no suitable use was found, and so the city council decided to sell it. Under the given economic conditions, this meant the certain demolition of the old museum building. In this situation, Eckhard Gerber courageously decided in 2013 to organize the celebration of his seventy-fifth birthday as possibly the last event in a building already approved for sale and demolition. For such a birthday celebration with a symposium and exhibition, there was indeed no better, more beautiful, and more impressive space available in the city than the atrium of the old Museum am Ostwall.
With brass instruments resonating downward from the heights of the gallery, the splendor of Saudi princes, and representatives from the mayor's office, this event reminded all participants that the roofed atrium was a magnificent event hall and that the old Museum am Ostwall was a dignified building and part of Dortmund's city history. This event thus became an important building block in making sure it was not the building's last.

Scene Four: The Ostwall and Archive Construction Sites

In the meantime, the idea had arisen to establish the Archiv für Architektur und Ingenieurbaukunst NRW of the TU Dortmund with a broader founda-

tion of supporters and to house it as the Baukunstarchiv NRW in the building of the former Museum am Ostwall. The path to realizing this vision was long and complicated, and in the course of these considerations the city had invited bids for a second expression of interest to sell the building in 2013. In order to prevent the outcome of only having applicants who were proposing to demolish and replace the building, Eckhard Gerber took the initiative to produce a design that would make it possible to preserve the old building while also using it as the Baukunstarchiv NRW.
With the aim of making this project economically viable for a private investor, Gerber expanded the design framework. Alongside the old Museum am Ostwall, he reconstructed the historical town plan and proposed a development based on the historical typology of town villas in place of the park from the postwar period. This made it possible to preserve most of the trees in the park, since they stood on what had previously been the gardens of the private properties. The idea was that the economic benefit from this city-center residential development would make it possible to use the old museum building for the Baukunstarchiv NRW in a largely cost-neutral way. The design was ingenious: fitting from an urban-planning point of view and historically well-founded. Yet it did not stand a chance, as the majority of the park was understandably regarded as sacrosanct. Despite this failure, however, Gerber was able to show that there were alternatives to the sale and demolition of the venerable building.

Scene Five: The Archive and Ostwall Construction Sites

After an alliance of the Architektenkammer NRW (NRW Chamber of Architects), the Ingenieurkammer-Bau NRW (NRW Chamber of Engineers), the Stiftung Deutscher Architekten (Foundation of German Architects), and the Förderverein für das Baukunstarchiv NRW (Friends of the Architectural Archive NRW) finally developed sustainable financing for the Baukunstarchiv NRW in cooperation with the TU Dortmund, Dortmund's city council decided in 2014 to offer the building of the former Museum am Ostwall to the Baukunstarchiv NRW and to renovate it with money from the state's urban development fund. Eckhard Gerber has been a member of the Förderverein since its inception in 2012 and played a decisive role as a driving force willing to take risks.
Since 2017, he has also served as the director of this association, which will continue to be tasked with cosponsoring the Baukunstarchiv. In doing so, he is making a significant contribution to permanently ensuring that the

Baukunstarchiv NRW will operate at the Ostwall in Dortmund. In the end, it was possible to solve two major problems by connecting two construction sites: the building at the Ostwall could be preserved, and this is also where the Baukunstarchiv NRW found a permanent home. Eckhard Gerber made a decisive contribution to both construction sites. The Baukunstarchiv NRW opened its doors in the fall of 2018—and there is thus no more beautiful and fitting place for Eckhard Gerber to celebrate his eightieth birthday. Thank you and congratulations!

Konzept+Atmosphäre Baukunstarchiv NRW, Dortmund—AIT Hamburg—Aedes Berlin

Dieter Nellen

Pictures and Models of an Exhibition

On his birthday in 2018, Eckhard Gerber was not without family and friends, public encounters, and cheerful company. Always active, he found it equally important to continue intellectual exchange about architecture and urban planning and to present projects from his office that are stylistically distinctive and currently coming to fruition.

The opening of the new Baukunstarchiv NRW (Architectural Archive of North Rhine-Westphalia) in the former Dortmund Museum Ostwall, which began hosting the Dortmunder Architekturtage under their first director, Josef Paul Kleihues, proved to be a fortunate circumstance. In the meantime, the building has become a discreetly elegant location for architecture—and incidentally, in the geographic center of the largest federal state in Germany. In the nineteenth century, the building—finished largely according to the historicist style of its time—initially served as the Prussian Mining Office for the burgeoning Montan region, and from 1911 onward as a museum of art and cultural history. After the destruction of the Second World War, the museum was rebuilt with a stylistic adaption of postwar modernism as a museum of modern art. In a relatively short period of time, it has now been suitably renovated for its new purpose, offering an ideal and material home for the architectural heritage of North-Rhine Westphalia. And here, in the heart of his decades-long adopted home Dortmund, on November 23, 2018, Eckhard Gerber publicly celebrated his eightieth birthday, still young as ever. At the same time, the first monographic exhibition presented by the new institution, the exhibition *Konzept+Atmosphäre,* was opened, showing works by Gerber Architekten. According to the press release, the exhibition aimed to ask: “How does an architectural idea become a site of emotion? How does architectural work appear in its abstract conceptual phase? How does the photographer’s gaze capture the concretely tangible spatial atmosphere that such a concept produces?”

The exhibition concept was not designed to be encyclopedic: its exposition is concentrated on concise or core messages. In a series of rooms, some suffused with daylight, it documented ten realized and six ongoing projects by Gerber Architekten. Gerber’s own residence, an example of contemporary building in the historical context of a former agricultural site with a villa and farmstead, was one of these works.

Konzept+Atmosphäre is at once a retrospective and contemporary show, as well as a reflective documentation on architectural photography as a medium. The selection of images was intended to paradigmatically make visible the design principles as programmatic narrative, and the iconographic possibilities, of architectural photography (most of which came from the Dortmund photographer Hans-Jürgen Landes). To quote the press release: the intention was to present “the harmonious-functional interplay of building and landscape, the special consideration of local contexts, and the light, the clarity that is characteristic of so many buildings constructed by the firm.”

The exhibition does not neglect the analog dimensions of presentations, either: the models on display, still testimonies to the authentic creativity of the architect, and still a visual reduction to the essence of a design, document the indispensable craftsmanship and existential dimension of architecture as a profession, despite its many digital aids. With their vivid simplicity and plausibility, these exhibited objects—which only appear to have fallen out of their time—remain important to Gerber and his architectural firm as evidence of professional expertise. Because without a good design, everything else is in vain.

After Dortmund, the exhibition devoted to Gerber Architekten traveled throughout Germany. Its next stops were the AIT Architecture Salon in Hamburg and the Architekturforum Aedes in Berlin with slight project variations and local references to Gerber’s offices in the cities on the Alster and the Spree.

Platforms of Discourse

In our media society, architecture lives not only from its built results. For its conceptual and visual exposition and acceptance, and in order to evaluate and develop itself, it must be accompanied by communication and

deepened by discourse—both internally and to the public. Gerber Architekten have thus added, to the succinct 2018/19 documentation of their work, topical discussions staged between Eckhard Gerber and prominent representatives of *Baukultur:* on November 23, 2018, with Volkwin Marg (gmp Architects), Gerber's eminent Hamburg colleague and traveling companion from their early days in Braunschweig (at the Technische Universität), about the commonalities of their profession and differences in the path that each of them took; on January 9, 2018, with Reiner Nagel, the Chairperson of the Bundesstiftung Baukultur (Federal Foundation of *Baukultur*), on the chances of success that *Baukultur* has for urbanity within the constraints of normative legislative or administrative provisions; and finally on February 20, 2019, with the Hamburg landscape architect Hinnerk Wehberg (WES LandschaftsArchitektur) on the dialectics of "architecture and urban space or open-air facilities" as well as each office's experiences with large projects.
The opening in the AIT Architecture Salon Hamburg took place on April 11, 2019, and consisted of an intellectual exchange between Eckhard Gerber and the colleagues and architectural partners of his Hamburg office, i. e., with representatives of the *next generation:* Jens Bentfeld and Hannes Beinhoff. Accordingly, the questions and topics raised by discussion leader Dr. Martin Tschechne followed the profile that Gerber Architekten has developed over the decades in its architecture and through its experience. These questions referred to the role of music, sound, and atmosphere as the "language" in and of architecture; respectively differing national architectural styles and differences in how they were accepted by clients in China and Saudi Arabia, as well as building globally in different cultural regions; the relationship between architecture, landscape, and urban interventions; and the dialectic of individualized architecture and possible brand development (by Gerber Architekten).
Finally, the last stop was the Architekturforum Aedes in Berlin, where Gerber Architekten organized a major exhibition of its work at the turn of 2016/17 on the occasion of its fiftieth anniversary. On this occasion, Kristin Feireiss and Beate Engelhorn left a note in the guestbook: "Fifty years of Gerber Architekten mean fifty years of using architecture and urban planning to develop and implement solutions for the challenges of a continuously changing world in an urban, regional, and global context." These words still apply today.

The Quality and Reflection of Building: *Baukultur* as an Art

Jörn Walter

The Ethics of the Master Builder

If one imagines the multitude of buildings and building tasks to which Eckhard Gerber has devoted himself over the decades, searching for a common core to his architecture, old-fashioned yet amazingly apt concepts such as morality and decency come to mind. Today, we would perhaps speak more of appropriateness, propriety, or aesthetic reason, but then we would surely do less justice to the work of Eckhard Gerber—both in its thoughtfulness and ethics on the one hand, and its poetry and beauty on the other. From the Harenberg high-rise to his offices in the Tönnishof, the King Fahad National Library to the Pfarrheim St. Ludgerus (St. Ludgerus Parish Hall), the Neue Messe Karlsruhe (New Karlsruhe Trade Fair and Exhibition Center), and his vacation home at the Karerpass, these projects are all sustained by an attitude that combines purpose and utility in architecture with creative intuition and design. This attitude aims to create places where one can spend time, and that are home, to respect origins and lifestyles, and finally to refine one's awareness and ethos. This is an architecture based on ethical principles, oriented toward people and places, which—in this social responsibility, as defined by Fritz Schumacher—we would no longer associate with the profession of the architect but with an older German word, the *Baumeister* or "master builder." Speaking about Eckhard Gerber means speaking about the ethics of the master builder.

Building is an art bound to a specific purpose. In 1965, Eckhard Gerber might have been able to attend Theodor W. Adorno's lecture at the Akademie der Künste (Academy of Arts), *Zum Problem des Funktionalismus heute* (translated by Jane O. Newman and John H. Smith as "Functionalism Today"), which argued that architecture is not primarily a field for personal expression but rather where this purpose allows "the tension between form and content which makes all artistic creation possible" to "communicate itself" in the first place. For architecture, this purpose is found in its function for subjects, users; it concerns architecture's responsibility toward society, its satisfaction in the present, and its hope for the future. It is based on an idea that has much in common with the Braunschweig school, where Eckhard Gerber studied. Here, the focus is on emphasizing the social responsibility of architecture for users and on the subject of architecture's significance for artistic creation—but its lessons also point a bit further. And indeed, Eckhard Gerber's buildings—whether large or small—share the quality of immediately making you feel at home, of radiating a sense of humanity and well-being and never conveying the feeling of mere habitation or cold splendor. Perhaps this elusive art in his work owes more to the pastor's house in which he grew up than it does to his education. Either way, there is no doubt that Gerber could identify with Adorno's thesis that "Architecture would thus attain a higher standard the more intensely it reciprocally mediated the two extremes—formal construction and function." This is a thesis that the Braunschweig school could have also claimed in the sense of design that is appropriately constructed and logically laid out and follows the rules of proportion and scale.

Eckhard Gerber succeeds in thus intertwining construction, utility, and beauty—at least to a degree that prompts not only admiration and fascination but also enthusiasm and euphoria. There is no question: we are talking here about an elevated kind of architecture, at the highest level, as can be conceived only by a true master builder. If an analogy to music is allowed, it is less related to the passion of classicism or the pathos of romanticism but rather to the harmonious balance between intellectual penetration and emotional creativity such as we find in Bach's Well-Tempered Clavier—systematic and disciplined, yet equally imaginative and inspired. Just think of the wonderful proportions of the windows in the Harenberg high-rise, the three-dimensional membrane construction providing protection from the sun at the King Fahad National Library, the cantilevered canopy of the Neue Messe Karlsruhe, the entrance atrium of the Dortmunder U that opens up all of the building's floors, the magnificent view of Magdeburg Cathedral through the showcase window of the Saxony-Anhalt state broadcasting building, the surprising play of colors of the residential buildings on Albermannstraße in Essen, the devotional transitions between the old and new buildings at the Hochschule für Musik und Theater (University of Music and Theater) in Leipzig or the floating cross in the chapel of the Raßnitz Jugendanstalt (Juvenile Detention Center). All of these are uplifting symbioses of poetry and objectivity, inspiration and reflection—at once touching and moving. They hint toward the promise of happiness we hope architecture might provide.

In pursuing the question of why such feelings arise when one regards this architecture, it becomes apparent this might have something to do with the way that Eckhard Gerber's work unconditionally concentrates on what is essential. There is no deception or pretense in his architecture; he is concerned with clarity and truth. For him, design has to do with reducing the numerous and ambiguous problems one always faces to their essence, with the ability to analyze, abstract, and synthesize. He is thus able to dispense with formal adventures, dalliances, and arbitrary or superfluous elements and find a path to achieve directness, restraint, simplicity, and clarity. This is a difficult and complex process, because it requires identifying what is essential before shaping it in a typical and specific way, revealing even more clearly why design is usually a quiet and sober-minded activity requiring a great deal of patience and endurance. But when these efforts are rewarded with buildings that strike us as entirely self-evident and familiar (even if we have never actually visited them), and that inspire us with new and surprising experiences of space—this is when we feel something of the significance of what is essential and what this means for architecture's promise for the future, a promise honored by so many of Eckhard Gerber's buildings.

This is also supported by the attitude of turning not only toward the building and its users, but also by fully paying attention to the urban surroundings and integrating construction into the landscape. Eckhard Gerber always focuses his view on the context in which his buildings stand. His architectural projects are always urban development projects, too. They fit in and at the same time bring out new experiences of the city and the natural environment. This is especially evident in looking at the Parish Center for the Johanniskirche (St. John's Church) in Witten, with its reference to the historical urban layout and its sense of proportionate scale; or the Niedersächsische Staats- und Universitätsbibliothek (Lower Saxony State and University Library) in Göttingen with its two faces, one turned toward the university and one toward the embankments ringing the old city; or the Kreishaus

(County Hall) in Vechta and the HAW Würzburg-Schweinfurt (University of Applied Sciences of Würzburg-Schweinfurt), with their elevated solutions based on permeability and visual relationships; or the floating cube of the Kunst- und Mediencampus Finkenau (Art and Media Campus Finkenau) and the representative buildings at the entrance of Gerber's global headquarters in Hamburg, with their choice of materials embedded in the neighborhood; and, of course, the urban planning for the Union Brewery complex in Dortmund and the outstandingly successful ensemble of its U Tower and vocational school. These buildings are all so appealing because they weave, almost casually, a highly sensitive and completely unlabored fabric of relationships to their surroundings, to the urban layout, topography, and green space, that appears as if it had come about on its own. Here, too, we see the tremendous power that can originate for design from the ability to analyze and abstract. Only those who possess this ability need not rely on historicizing imitation, and vice versa.

Hence the source of Eckhard Gerber's architectural language quite clearly springs from the constantly evolving stages of modernity, or rather from current events and the current state of development. From Bauhaus modernism, his work has taken objectivity and functionality; from postwar modernism, modesty and lightness; and from the self-reflexivity of modernity, thoughtfulness and the skill for integration. These are the creative sources that have allowed him to find his own way of designing: unobtrusive, open, and undogmatic. His numerous buildings show individual faces but follow a common thread. The more deeply one engages with this work, the more obvious one thing becomes: "what is crucial in the consideration of architecture is not seeing but the apprehension of structures. The objective effect of the buildings on the imaginative being of the viewer is more important than their 'being seen.'" Eckhard Gerber entered into this sphere, described by Walter Benjamin in his 1933 review *Kunstwissenschaftliche Forschungen* (translated by Thomas Y. Levin), early on and has basically never strayed from the direction it set out. I offer admiration and respect for anyone who can say that about themselves. And who can thus also meet any social changes, technological innovations, and artistic currents with a conscious and curious mind, without having to deform themselves. And who, for this reason, will always find his breath taken away by the exciting aspects of their profession. In a word, Eckhard Gerber is a master builder who values aesthetics—and even more so, who values ethics.

Architecture, Urban Space, Landscape

Dieter Nellen and Christa Reicher in dialogue with Eckhard Gerber

Green Spaces and Open Spaces as Building Blocks of Urbanity

The understanding of open space and landscape in relation to built structure has changed in recent decades: the traditional notion of landscape as complementary to the built city seems obsolete. Green spaces and open spaces are functionally more than what development has left over and open, and also more than something that might serve as ecological compensation or territorial decoration.

Cityscape and landscape have long since ceased to be classic antagonists, having become different forms of expression of the way in which our environment is culturally shaped. Ideally, shaped nature joins with architecture and urban space on an equal footing. It can—as a garden, park, or landscape—indeed be "a city by other means."

It thus only makes sense to regard landscape, too, as a building block of urbanity and use it accordingly in the process of design. Sometimes, the landscape even provides the creative key for future design: in large industrial-cultural conversion projects, urban development designs follow the character of the landscape in which they are located. They take up the autonomous force of development inherent to the landscape and use it for spatial design.

In Germany and Europe, there are excellent offices for landscape and open space planning that have emancipated themselves from the classical disciplines of architecture, urban planning, and structural engineering, to have since established a relationship on equal footing. They now jointly design and act as equal partners in competitions and tenders.

Architectural Noblesse and Shaped Landscape

Architecture and topography can form a harmonious symbiosis of architectural noblesse and shaped landscape. Contemporary museums in particular are situated directly in relation to parks, defined by an optical dialectic of art inside and nature outside. One thinks here of the Museum Angewandte Kunst in Frankfurt (directly on the Main) and the Museum Frieder Burda in Baden-Baden, both of which are creations of the American architect Richard Meier, or—somewhat less spectacularly—the Lehmbruck Museum in Duisburg or the Josef Albers Museum Quadrat Bottrop. Other spaces for art, such as the Arp Museum Bahnhof Rolandseck am Rhein, the Langen Foundation by Tadao Ando, and the Museum Insel Hombroich by Erwin Heerich in Neuss, convey a harmonious interplay of architecture and a cultural landscape that provides a source of identity.

Parks and Industrial Landscapes

Contemporary industrial parks, too, are designed less often with true parks or landscapes than with peripheral green backdrops. They seek their urban autonomy in the harmonious texture of architecture, gardens, and park landscape as a comprehensive spatial framework, such as one sees in the design by Hamburg landscape architect Hinnerk Wehberg for the Autostadt Wolfsburg.

Architecture needs outside space as a constitutive element: the projected new buildings for the corporate headquarters of the American communications industry are often described in reviews as inward-looking work landscapes and park landscapes of the near future. They are not skyscrapers (anymore), or architectural statements of hegemony and universal demands. Rather, Norman Foster's designs for Apple and Frank O. Gehry's for Facebook deliberately dispense with architectural dominance and are conspicuously understated in contrast to the actual power of their clients. The flat architectural structures for communication and creativity, with their huge horizontal surfaces, virtually take cover within an artificial park landscape, simulating nature as the backdrop and imagination of a historically stylized environment.

Architecture, Urban Space, and Landscape by Eckhard Gerber

The way in which landscape can be deployed in architecture and urban planning varies, depending on the building task itself, user specifications, and the situation of the site, which is always unique. The aim is to create a

close link between open space and built environment; a kind of symbiosis in which both complement each other to form an interwoven unity. In the same way, open space, landscape, and the built environment can create a special tension between each other.
Architecture must therefore always have landscape and urban space in mind, just as landscape and urban space should also always be thinking of architecture. This has consequences for architecture (and vice versa).

How much shaping does natural open space need?
Gerber: As little as possible when dealing with an untouched natural setting, or with landscape, or, on the other hand, a strong design might be necessary when the situation and the task require it or make it sensible.
Dealing with landscapes and open space requires a high degree of sensitivity and, even more than architecture, is a quite artistic task. Compared to architecture, it is freer from functional and technical constraints. We often speak of landscape paintings—this terminology obviously reflects an artistic approach.

What do landscape and urban space mean to you and your team in your own architecture?
Gerber: We do not see architecture as something detached, but as a totality with landscape and urban space. Our concepts always constitute a whole; they are always conceived from this unity of urban space, architecture, and landscape. In this respect, our design approaches are always based on a deep desire for a close connection between architecture and landscape, interior and exterior space.
Urban space is the result of architecture, and for this reason it cannot be viewed in isolation or separately anyway. We always develop complete concepts for our projects based on this conviction. We do so with our own landscape architecture team, which I built up in the 1970s and which is an integral part of our work. However, we only work on the landscape spaces for our own projects; we don't carry out landscape planning for projects of other architects.

Can you think of particularly striking contemporary examples of the symbiosis of architecture, park, and landscape?
Gerber: Of course, for example the Kurhaus in Badenweiler, which is integrated into a wonderful park. It stands on a hill, which grows to become a mountain, on top of which stands a castle ruin made of rock—as a crown, so to speak. The building of the Kurhaus consists of floating floors stacked on top

of each other and pushed up against the slope, providing a panoramic view of the landscape from within. The staggered roof surfaces, which push out of the slope, as it were, are terraces and green spaces, so the building itself becomes a landscape.

And across all of the floors, a staircase develops along the slope from the lowest entrance level through the hall, which is as tall as the entire building, with a view looking up toward to the castle. The natural stone staircase built into the slope thus becomes part of the castle and suggests that the castle is growing upward from the Kurhaus—an incredible unity of this new building, the landscape, and the existing structures.

Another, much more well-known example, is the Olympic Park in Munich designed by Günter Behnisch, Fritz Auer, and Carlo Weber. The entire structural concept, with stadium, indoor swimming pool, and sports hall and spectator grandstands for each of these, consists of a landscaped terrain over which tent roofs have been stretched, which also provide cover for open spaces. This is one of the most intimate connections of building and landscape that I know. The canal was extended to the lake, and the excavated material was used to shape the terrain while the rubble of the war debris was also used in the landscaping, and as a sign of the past.

This was a very smart way of expressing the Olympic games in postwar Germany: playful, free, open, and unpretentious. A contrast to the power-demonstrating games in the Third Reich in 1936! A splendid statement! For me, this design is an unsurpassed classic in its wonderful combination of building and landscape.

Which projects of this kind would you cite as exemplary for your own work?

Gerber: As already mentioned, we have engaged in landscape planning since the 1970s in order to develop and realize this interplay of building and landscape as an overall concept. One of our early pioneer projects (1974 to 1981) was the city hall in Hagen, where the building ensemble forms the structural reference point for a historical quarry, and its visual presence almost physically protrudes into the building; or the second training center [we built] in Münster, where the building and landscape are closely interwoven. This is also the case for the administration center in Leipzig with the inclusion of an old alley of chestnut trees.

A very current example is the competition we won in 2017 for Allianz-Versicherung in Stuttgart. The design creates translucent spatial experiences within its so-called new working environments represented by the diversity of views into the courtyards, which have been heavily planted, as well as into the surrounding landscape and the whole ensemble. The architecture is part of the landscape, and the landscape is part of the architecture, which also uses a 150-year-old oak tree to formulate the transition from the urban space to the space of the landscape.

Which personal memories of history and landscape do you owe to the smaller town where you grew up and to the landscape of your childhood home in Thuringia?
Gerber: First, of course, the Wartburg Castle as a building that shapes this cultural landscape in central Germany, with its special significance for the German Reformation and intellectual history. For more private worlds of family and intimate friends, what left a formative impact was my own hometown with its dense village structure, its order, and natural delimitation from and fusion with the surrounding landscape.

As you described it, your own office always thinks architecture and open space planning in a single context. Does this not inevitably lead to the dominance of architectural design criteria and to the instrumentalization of outside space, to outside space having a decorative function?
Gerber: No, on the contrary—added value results if you make the most of the autonomy and interdependence of the two areas. Working from one creative vision, together in a team, generates synergy effects in terms of content; this doesn't lead at all to an imbalance, as our work consistently proves. For particularly large projects, however, we sometimes like to work together with other landscape planners, such as WES or Rainer Schmidt for the large Central Park in Riyadh.

What conceptual attitude determines your approach in this process?
Gerber: Our works show that we consistently have different attitudes and approaches in dealing with the landscape, such as thinking the existing landscape further as a conceptual approach; continuing to build on the existing landscape, architecture and urban structure as a whole; landscape with topography as a rationale for the architectonic positioning; the building as a mediator and boundary between built urban structure and landscape; the creation of new landscape; and so on.

Your own residence and office building is located in a green area in the semi-urban surroundings of a district of Dortmund, with a villa from the *Gründerzeit* and a historic stable and barn building. Was this preference a coincidence, a professional opportunity, and/or a programmatic decision?

Gerber: It started as a lucky coincidence and then became a programmatic statement. The green area in Dortmund-Kley, which runs along the Feldbach from Dorney to the north, is a tree-covered green corridor that was once part of a large contiguous agricultural area but has now unfortunately been converted into industrial sites. Our Tönnishof is situated on a remnant of this green space and stands as an oasis in the nondescript commercial monotony of the surroundings, which were developed in the 1980s.

[This historic building] can still surprise you, as with so many similar green oases in the Ruhr region, which is in fact quite green [despite its reputation]. Our Tönnishof in Dortmund-Kley, as an existing building with only minor interventions, thus became a beautiful example of the success and effect of the unity of combining building and landscape, and the peace this radiates out to the people who live and work here.

The Passion of Building On

Falk Jaeger

On Eckhard Gerber's Engagement with Historical Buildings

Architects usually see themselves as the generalists of their discipline. Eckhard Gerber, too, finds it hard to limit himself to one area of construction. That said, over the course of his many years of creative work, focal points have emerged, such as office or university construction. Yet regardless of whether he is designing apartments, offices, churches, libraries, factories, or recreational facilities, whether he is planning buildings for science and teaching, for art or culture—in his view, the architect is essentially a universal artist capable of taking on any commission.

Historic preservation, conversion, and building in historical surroundings, for example, is one construction sector that is becoming increasingly important because of the scarcity of building land and resources. This is doubtless a field with competent, well-known specialists. Some of them aim to secure and preserve the substance of historical buildings entrusted to their care without making any compromises. And some of them consider the original substance of a building to be sacred, aiming to preserve it for posterity under any circumstances. Eckhard Gerber, however, does not belong to these dogmatic monument preservationists.

Instead, he attempts to retrace the essence of a historical building, to grasp its idiosyncrasies and qualities. "One must accept such a monument and identify with it. The more intensely this happens, the less one can hurt it, as far as its existence is concerned," he says. What Gerber does believe a monument can bear, however, is the continuation of its construction—absorption by a new context, supplementation by something new. He sees the present-day existence of a monument not as a final state to be preserved but as a stage in its life within a larger (architectural) historical context, reaching into the present and continuing into the future. From this position, there is no legitimacy in looking back to an earlier epoch, in reconstructing a lost state.

Gerber's engagement with the former brewery building of the Dortmunder Union, commonly called the Dortmunder U, is a particularly vivid illustration of how such a procedure might look. Renovation, conversion, extension: what should we call it? It's a little bit of everything. We're talking about a fortress-like brick building west of the main railway station in Dortmund, with a monumental, six-meter-high, gold-plated U on top that shines far and wide. Built in 1927 as the central fermenting and cellar tower of the Union brewery, the building had over time become a symbol of the local brewing industry: a rather unsightly complex of buildings, its bricks cracked and falling apart, a solitary structure amid the industrial wasteland at the edge of the city center.

Since its renovation, a colorful mix of cultural and creative industries has found its place in the tower. Gerber Architekten won the architectural competition to convert the industrial shell, in collaboration with Professor Gernot Schulz, and then took over the further development and realization of the project. Turning the building, which was divided into stacked floors, into a functioning cultural center was no easy task. For Eckhard Gerber, the bold measure of ripping out the first row of ceiling sections along the east side of all the building's floors in order to gain a hall, as high as the building, along the outer wall and floors—what he called the *Kunstvertikale* or "art vertical"—was a "small surgical intervention with great effect." It serves to open up the space and allow visitors to experience the dimensions and presence of the historical building. This is a creative, though not hypersensitive, way of dealing with this monument of a building that gives it an unforeseen effect. Heading upwards in the building on the escalator, in the space between the historic façade and the modern floors supported by powerful concrete pillars and ceiling beams, becomes a special architectural experience.

Even with the additions and bay windows that cut through the outer wall, Gerber has asserted himself in opposition to historic preservationist positions. "The transformation of the brewery building into a house of art should also become clear externally," he explained. The bay windows bring more light into the interior and offer space for special functions, such as the VIP lounge, which juts forth from the fourth upper floor as a lookout from

the façade, or the two-storey library on the fifth upper floor, which cantilevers out of the building.
The first two upper floors, which provide space for Dortmund's universities and the Center for Cultural Education, have halls in their center supported by columns that can be used for a myriad of purposes, surrounded by peripheral offices and conference rooms. The floor used by the art association Hartware MedienKunstVerein HMKV is kept free of further interior construction and is only temporarily subdivided and used for media installations.
The higher rooms above, reaching almost six meters from floor to ceiling, are the new home of the Museum am Ostwall (Museum Ostwall). The entrance forms a two-storey hall connecting both floors in the southern part of the tower, which makes it easier for visitors to orient themselves. On the top floor a spacious skylight hall for temporary exhibitions has a surprising effect. By raising the roof, the architects saw the opportunity to create a column-free hall of a size that does not otherwise exist in the building—a self-confident, pragmatic act of appropriating the monument. Under the roof of the tower, one finds a special attraction called the Cathedral. Here, the architect used the visual appeal of the historical construction to give a special aura to the panoramic restaurant VIEW, which functions as a prominent location for cultural events and club activities until late into the night.
The Dortmunder U is a stroke of luck because it succeeded in allowing a monument important for the identity of the city to speak for itself, and in securing its continued existence through high-quality, intensive use.
By contrast, one could describe Gerber's approach to the headquarters of the Volksbank in Dortmund as the use of historical building substance as a mass ready to be shaped, rather than as historic preservation. Eckhard Gerber's suggested solution was not to demolish the existing building from the 1960s but rather to integrate it into the new project. Yet the existing architecture retained its characteristics and was mirrored, as it were, by a second L-shaped wing. In between, covered with a bold flying roof, a glass hall was created as a transitory space with a connection to the network of paths found in the surrounding urban structure. This represents an adaptation of what already existed on the site and a creative reinterpretation of the location as it was found.
Gerber's credo: "An old building can hold many starting points and challenges for a new whole. Thus, one often achieves something much better than one would with demolition and an entirely new construction." This was also his guiding principle for the entrance to the company building

of Wilo, which Gerber inserted between two older buildings. The aim was to articulate the contrast between old and new while creating a harmonious overall building through the prominently protruding glass wedge of the staircase, with the new addition also sending a clear, recognizable signal for the newly designed entrance.

As with many historical buildings during GDR times, the Preußische Geologische Landesanstalt (Prussian Geological Office) from the 1870s was treated roughly—subjected to a rather heavy-handed renovation for use by the Ministry of Geology. Yet the building offered an impressive structure and high-quality details that were worth reviving. The task was thus to remove many structures that had been internally added and undo changes—for example, by stripping the pillars, which were too thick and concealed charming old columns; or revitalizing the large atrium, with its two-storey gallery balconies (building type: caravansary); or redesigning the offices, allowing their vaulted ceilings to once again achieve their effect with partitions glazed at the top. The architect Max Dudler was responsible for implementing the renovation concept and realizing the newly built additions.

For the concert hall of the Hochschule für Musik und Theater (University of Music and Theater) in Leipzig, built at the same time, Eckhard Gerber emphasized contrast. Here, the task was to make complete again a Wilhelminian three-wing complex from 1887, whose southern wing had been destroyed during the war. The construction site in the interior of the block made it possible to take sweeping design liberties without impinging on the historical building. A new, stylistically independent building reflecting the contemporary moment was created, with orange-brown panel façades and glass walls. The main focus in dealing with the existing building was on establishing distance between old and new through glass joints and bridges, following the principle of "self-confident dialogue instead of pandering."

The Rudolf Virchow Center at the Universität Würzburg (University of Würzburg) was also handled in a way that respected and enhanced the existing structure. The former surgical ward of the Luitpold Hospital—an L-shaped historic building in baroque forms—was completely renovated and given a new roof. The elongated new building, arranged parallel to the north side, created an inner courtyard divided by a central auditorium. The western courtyard area became the internal garden courtyard, and the eastern courtyard became a glass-roofed atrium—a hall meant to open up the building and foster communication, in which the historical outer façades of the east and south wings are presented as if they were objects in an exhibition.

Once again, the old building was treated respectfully and given a new effect, even though the new buildings are uncompromisingly modern in design and the contact points between old and new are executed as glass connections that create distance.
Whether in projects as diverse as the conversion of the Tönnishof stable building in 1884 and the expansion of the associated country house into Gerber's own architectural office in Dortmund, or the new King Fahad National Library in Riyadh, which included integrating an existing building from the 1970s, one repeatedly encounters this friendly-yet-distanced attitude toward historical heritage in Gerber's work. Though it is appreciated and cultivated, this heritage is never accepted as a binding blueprint for additions and conversions but is rather self-confidently supplemented by something new. This is a masterful way of building on by later generations, as it was already practiced in early epochs.

Ideas and Interventions: Building with Art

Rouven Lotz

A prominent early work by Eckhard Gerber, the city hall in Hagen completed in 1981, is, retrospectively, already groundbreaking for the architect's overall architectural oeuvre. Gerber and his competition partners from Hagen and Meschede were able to win the tender on the basis of a surprising concept. Instead of placing the building in the middle of the rocky landscape created by the abandoned limestone quarry, as stipulated in the competition tender, Eckhard Gerber recommended situating it at the outer edge of the site. This not only made it possible to use the oval landscape of the quarry as a rock garden. Continuing the quarry's striking topography made the building an urban landmark with a visual relation to the city center. The glass skin of the building contrasts with the rocky landscape designed by the landscape planner Georg Penker (based in Neuss) and, at the same time, recalls the original use of the building site. Nearly four decades later, the overall concept has proven to be especially fortunate for wildlife in Hagen. But from the outset, the city hall building itself—a public construction contract—was intended to be equipped with works of art. The municipal planning official at the time, Herbert Böhme, and Gerber agreed on works from two artists, without staging a competition: the sculptor Jürgen Weber (1928–2007) from Braunschweig and the painter Emil Schumacher (1912–1999) from Hagen. Even then, Gerber pursued the concept of relating interior and exterior space to one another. This also influenced the selection of the artwork chosen for the building. For the exterior space, Gerber suggested the sculptor, whose design for a bronze sculpture with larger-than-life figurative elements entitled *Windsbräute* (Windsbrides) (height: 4.6 meters) was finally acquired in 1984 after difficult disputes between the city and the artist.

It was then integrated into a fountain constructed using the paving of the forecourt and the limestone rock extracted on site during the preparations for the building site. As was already the case for the landscape planning, a solution was also favored for the fountain that forms a clear contrast to the geometric structures. For the interior, allegorical majolica putti from the historic town hall (built in the early twentieth-century during the so-called Hagen impulse) were planned. In addition, a test mosaic (*Die Lautenspielerin,* or Lute Player, 138.5 × 128.5 centimeters), which the artist Johan Thorn Prikker had created in 1914 thanks to the involvement of Karl Ernst Osthaus as decoration for the chamber music hall in the previous building, was hung in a prominent place. The original town hall from 1914 (completed only in 1922 because of the war) stood not far from the new building but was demolished in the wake of the Second World War. The decoration of the new building with works of art from its predecessor, whose sculptural façade by expressionist sculptors Milly Steger and Will Lammert was destroyed during the demolition of the building in 1954, still represents an important symbolic link for the Hagen public today. In addition, a large-format painting by Emil Schumacher was to be acquired as the highlight of the artworks for the building's interior. The painter, from Hagen, had been one of the most important international representatives of contemporary German art since the 1950s. Both the architect and the painter were enthusiastic about the idea of the head of the city planning office, Böhme, to each contribute a work for the city hall. And both artists very much regretted the fact that an acquisition did not ultimately come about. The painting is a major work from this creative phase and today part of the collection of the Emil Schumacher Museum, because the artist did not later make it available for sale to other buyers.

About fifteen years later, a successful collaboration nevertheless did take shape when Gerber asked the painter to contribute the design of a ceramic wall for the new building of the employment office in Dortmund. Although Gerber did not specifically build up a private art collection but rather surrounded himself with personal favorites, Schumacher exemplifies the persistence with which Gerber acts—similar to an ambitious art collector—in advocating for the artists involved in his projects while also taking care in his private sphere to maintain connections he makes in the course of this work. If one is lucky enough to be invited to the Gerber family's private home, one might see the host open a large cupboard in the kitchen and reveal porcelain with decor designed by Emil Schumacher. Above all, however, through this art in architecture Gerber has permanently inscribed his architectural oeuvre with his thoroughly personal collection of art.

Art in Architecture—Every Word Is One Too Many

Art in architecture had already fallen into disrepute in several respects when the young architect Eckhard Gerber won and implemented his first competitions for prominent public building projects. For centuries, up to the Baroque era, it was a given that art would be included in representative buildings, both sacred and secular. The organization of the medieval mason's lodge, for example, did not did not consider architecture and sculpture to be separate. Master builders were also experienced stonemasons, and it was this unity that made Gothic cathedrals possible in the first place. In modern times, sculpture became separate from architecture, as did painting: both disciplines were now perceived as independent liberal arts alongside architecture. With the industrialization during the nineteenth century, which also affected the building trade, master masons and architects were finally able to turn to early industrial production for decorative elements. The counterdevelopment of the reform art from the turn of the century once again connected these aspects in the phenomenon of so-called artist architects and the Gesamtkunstwerk. After the short beacon of Art Nouveau, however, a tremendous objectification in architecture took place, for which the Bauhaus is today regarded as the most famous point of reference.

From the 1910s onwards, progressive architecture increasingly dispensed with architectural decoration. The creations of architecture as an applied artistic discipline themselves became works of art—partly leading in the period that followed, through an entirely false interpretation, to a complete suppression of works by independent artists. As early as 1908, Adolf Loos commented about the ornament: "it is a crime against the national economy that human labor, money, and material are thereby destroyed. Time cannot compensate for this damage."[1] Loos's attitude to ornamentation does not refer to art in architecture, but it can be transferred to the criticism of the 1970s, when—in addition to the role of propaganda art in National Socialism—in particular the original social aspect of welfare for artists was rejected. The history of art in architecture began shortly before the world economic crisis in the Weimar Republic, when the Reichswirtschaftsverband bildender Künstler Deutschlands (German Imperial Trade Association of Visual Artists) encouraged artists to take part in state building projects in order to

1 Adolf Loos, "Ornament und Verbrechen," 1908, in Adolf Loos, *Sämtliche Schriften in zwei Bänden*, vol. 1, edited by Franz Glück (Vienna: Herold, 1962), 276–288.

Hagen city hall, *Windsbräute*, fountain sculpture by Jürgen Weber, 1984

Emil Schumacher, *MIDUN*, 1975, oil on wood, 197 × 200 cm, currently in the collection of the Emil Schumacher Museum in Hagen

provide them with economic support through commissions. What initially emerged as a social idea to combat poverty was soon recognized by the great state powers of the time as an effective means of propaganda. Against the backdrop of social support for artists, the selection of artworks (in the immediate reconstruction period), which was at times comparatively uncritical, was cited in debates of the 1970s as general proof that in the meantime promoting art in architecture had only come to conceal the empty content of investment art, and that art in architecture was thus again being abused, albeit with a new purpose.[2]

More than twenty years after the program of art in architecture was confirmed as an integral part of the reconstruction of the Federal Republic of Germany following the Second World War, questions were raised about whether it made sense to continue it as a state-sponsored building task. At this time, however, the Deutsche Städtetag (German Association of Cities) issued recommendations on art and architecture whose arguments can still be regarded as generally valid today, and for Gerber's oeuvre in particular: "the city should be a place that enables socialization and communication. It should encourage individuals to think and act creatively. This requires that not only sober functionality but also artistic intention be incorporated as an element into urban development."[3] Moreover, massive changes in questions about art in general, as well as the prevalence of new media that had until then played only a subordinate role (such as video, sound, or performance art), made it necessary to examine the applicability of these forms of art in architecture. Numerous symposia, lectures, studies, and publications have increasingly dealt with questions on this topic. By contrast, the influential architectural historian Julius Posener (1904–1996) wrote in the monthly journal of the Deutscher Werkbund, *Werk und Zeit:* "Every word said about 'art in architecture' is one too many."[4]

The Architect as Collector

Looking back, the intense but unresolved confrontation between different perspectives shows the relevance of the topic for the younger generation in the mid-1970s. The retrospective of Eckhard Gerber's architectural body of work impressively documents how the architect considered art in architecture to be a self-evident aspect of his building activity. Among Gerber's first projects are schools and universities such as in Siegen (1973–1976), bank buildings (1969–1973), the city hall in Hagen mentioned above (1974–1981), the Bildungszentrum der Bundesfinanzverwaltung (Training Center

2 Marianne and Roland Günther, "Die verbaute Kunst: 'Kunst am Bau' oder Bau als Kunst—zum Verlust benutzbarer Architektur," *Werk und Zeit, Monatszeitung für Umweltgestaltung*, Deutscher Werkbund (ed.), no. 23, issue 8/9 (August/September 1974): 1.

3 Eberhard Harms, *Kunst in der Architektur: 25 Jahre künstlerisches Schaffen im staatlichen Hochbau in Baden-Württemberg* (Stuttgart: Finanzministerium Baden-Württemberg, 1979), 8–9.

4 Julius Posener, "Was ist funktionalistisch?" *Werk und Zeit, Monatszeitung für Umweltgestaltung*, Deutscher Werkbund (ed.), no. 23, issue 8/9 (August/September 1974): 2.

of the Federal Finance Administration) in Münster (1976–1987), and the city rail stop Stadtgarten in Dortmund, including the design for the surrounding city square (1979–1982). In particular, the city hall in Hagen and the city rail stop in Dortmund are examples of the great importance that Gerber's basic architectural approach places on having a holistic urban environmental design, which includes integrating the aims of art in architecture from the outset. Subsequent projects created as buildings for private clients, such as the Harenberg high-rise (1993) or the RWE Tower (2005) with its own exhibition area in Dortmund's city center, prove the continuing importance of art in architecture for Eckhard Gerber, even beyond the influence exerted by the legally mandated percentage quota for investment in art in public projects.

The collection of contemporary art gradually created by Gerber in his building projects documents a broad spectrum of works within the genres of sculpture and painting. This can be illustrated with several examples, such as the fountain of jesters by sculptor Eberhard Linke (*1937), which already appears as an integral part of the overall design of the Stadtgarten city rail stop that was built in 1982. During a stay in the Villa Massimo in Rome, Linke designed a fountain for the above-ground design of the city square in close coordination with the plans for the train stop that were just taking shape. No specifications had been made in the tender. It was not with a completely independent contribution but rather through a sculptural reaction to the newly emerging site that Linke convinced the jury. Through an interplay with the glass garden pavilion, he developed the fountain of jesters in the immediate vicinity of the Dortmund City Hall by continuing the architectural wall elements of the building for the underground station, thus supporting the linking of building and landscape with his work. Analogous to the architectural design, Linke's fountain also reacts to the extreme gradient of the building site. Larger-than-life-sized bronze figures that are part of the fountain also establish a direct relationship to passers-by in the urban space. The Bildungszentrum der Bundesfinanzverwaltung in Münster, completed in 1987, is home to a large number of works by visual artists, prominent among them sculptures by Linke and Hubertus von Pilgrim (*1931) as well as paintings by Pitt Moog (1932–2017). With paintings covering more than forty columns and ceilings, Moog left his mark on the entire building complex. For the Niedersächsische Staats- und Universitätsbibliothek (Lower Saxony State and University Library) in Göttingen, opened in 1993, it was possible to engage the sculptor Erich Reusch (*1925). With his work *Grüne Säule* (Green Pillar) (lacquered aluminum, height: 15 meters, incline: 7 degrees, 1992), Reusch created an intervention into the external space visible from far away. For the Harenberg City Center (HCC, 1993) and the Dortmund employment office (1995), which is now the Agentur für Arbeit (Employment Agency), outdoor sculptures by the kinetic artist George Rickey (1907–2002) were acquired. As with the private building project of the HCC (Bodo Harenberg), the client for this public project (the Bundesanstalt für Arbeit) played an important role in the decision-making process for the art chosen for this architecture. From the very beginning, the client deliberately forewent a competition and sought out already established artistic positions for the new building. For example, the idea to acquire works by George Rickey for outdoor use came from the client. Two works were acquired during a visit with the sculptor, who was more than eighty years old at the time. When one of the two sculptures was completed before the building, it was initially installed in the Stadewäldchen park in Dortmund. In 1990, a first exhibition of Rickey's works had already taken place at the internationally active Galerie Utermann in Dortmund. When the publisher Bodo Harenberg had a new publishing house designed and built by Gerber at a prominent location in Dortmund's city center, a sculpture garden was also created for the outside area of the project. Wilfried Utermann organized the opening of this garden on Harenberg's behalf with an exhibition of Rickey's sculptures. A sculpture of four floating, stainless steel cubes of the same size, *Cluster of Cubes* (1991, height: 3.75 meters), was also acquired as permanent art for the building (though it has since been uninstalled). The sculptures *Broken Column* (1993, height: 5.5 meters) and *Triangles Horizontal Jointed* (1995, 4.0 × 4.2 × 0.8 meters), also previously acquired and installed in the Stadewäldchen park, had not yet been placed in their final location in the working area of what was, at the time, the Dortmund employment office. They were installed in this location only in 1995. The high towering sculpture *Broken Column* consists of a triple broken square pillar made of stainless steel, the limbs of which move, as if weightless, in opposite directions in the wind. *Triangles Horizontal Jointed* lies flat, elevated above ground level, over a shallow surface of water. It consists of three unevenly sized, triangular elements that are arranged horizontally and move independently of each other. Following Gerber's suggestion, Emil Schumacher designed a ceramic wall (1995) for the interior of the Dortmund employment office, located centrally in the building and cutting across two floors

Exterior view of the building for the Bildungs- und Wissenschafts-zentrum der Bundesfinanzverwaltung in Münster, with the sculpture *Matthäusbrücke* by Eberhard Linke, 1987

Cluster of Cubes/Gruppe aus vier Würfeln by George Rickey at the square in front of the entrance to the Harenberg high-rise, Dortmund

Fountain of jesters by Eberhard Linke as a part of the Stadtgarten city rail stop, Dortmund, 1982

as a flanking wall of a staircase. The front and back were painted with gesturally abstract compositions (128 ceramic basalt tiles, 6.0 × 8.0 meters). Both sides of the wall are late works of the painter showing the figurative ciphers typical of his work since the 1980s, within an abstract composition. The linear forms on the inner surface are reminiscent of a horizon line as well as the protective motif of the house.[5] With an implied monumental wheel motif on the outward-facing side, which can be interpreted as a symbol of work and technology, Emil Schumacher has nevertheless created a direct reference to the building's purpose.[6] In this context, Eckhard Gerber stresses that he considers it important to perceive the entire wall as a spatial body, similar to a sculpture. The ceramic wall itself is also an example of the connection between inside and outside in Gerber's architectural work. Installed close behind the glass façade, it is also visible from the outside when suitably lit.[7]
In many cases today, as in Eckhard Gerber's architectural work, art in architecture is integrated into buildings that have already been planned or erected. In 1990, however, Gerber expressed the following observation on the relationship between art and architecture for a publication on Pitt Moog: "Today, art, also in connection with architecture, is independent, self-confident, existing through itself—more the antithesis of architecture. It is the autonomy of the contrast this produces out of which we must today seek to formulate the connection between the fields off architecture and art. Art and architecture thus acquire a new dimension in their connection with each other, the meaning of which lies in developing contents from the nexus of their polarity."[8] Gerber finds an ideal historical example of a partnership between an architect and an independent artist in the cooperation of the brothers Cosmas Damian Asam (1686–1739) and Egid Quirin Asam (1692–1750), whose joint works are regarded as highlights of the late Baroque period in southern Germany. For Gerber, the Asam brothers are exemplary for such a connection. In his view, their collaboration gave rise to a unique creation that would not have been possible without the cooperation of both artists, ultimately resulting in a Gesamtkunstwerk.[9] Gerber writes about this ideal: "Such a result can only emerge from an intentional, desired collaboration between architect and artist who are together capable of finding the unified whole within polarity."[10] Because of this attitude, he thus also gives the artists involved in his building projects as much space as possible to develop an autonomous effect of their own work. In the best cases, such as in numerous buildings of Gerber's, in the employment office in Dortmund or the Bildungszentrum der Bundesfinanzverwaltung in Münster, the building

5 See Ulrich Schumacher and Rouven Lotz, *Emil Schumacher: Blätter aus dem Engadin* (Dortmund: Verlag Kettler, 2019), as well as Ulrich Schumacher and Rouven Lotz, *Emil Schumacher: Orte der Geborgenheit* (Dortmund: Verlag Kettler, 2017).

6 See Ulrich Schumacher and Rouven Lotz, *Emil Schumacher: Räder: Werk* (Dortmund, Verlag Kettler, 2018).

7 Personal statement by Eckhard Gerber in a conversation with Rouven Lotz in April 2019; additional discussions took place in November 2017 and February 2019, as well as on other dates. The author owes a debt of thanks to Eckhard Gerber for numerous references used in writing this essay.

8 Eckhard Gerber, "Kunst und Architektur," in *Pitt Moog: 1986–1990; Ausstellungskatalog anlässlich einer Wanderausstellung in zahlreichen Städten Europas*, edited by Pitt Moog et al. (Hildesheim: Hildesheimer Druck- und Verl.-GmbH, 1900), 63–64.

9 Personal communication, April 2019.

10 Gerber, "Kunst und Architektur," 64.

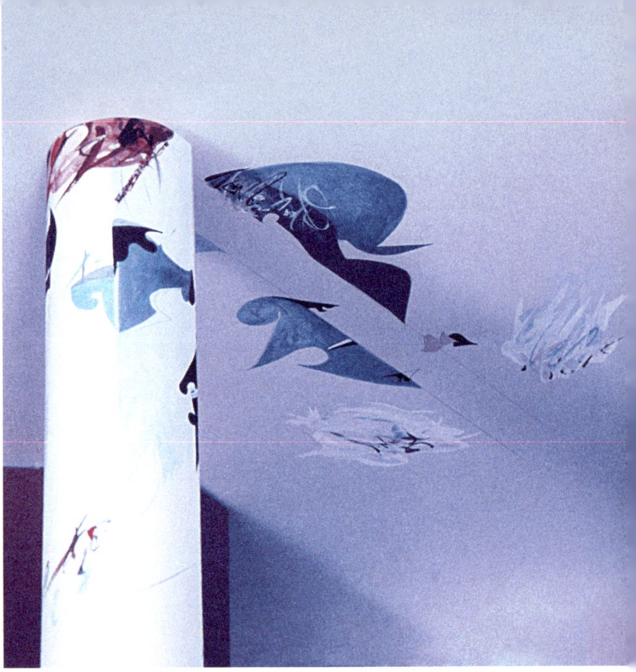

Paintings by Pitt Moog in the Bildungs- und Wissenschaftszentrum der Bundesfinanzverwaltung in Münster, 1987

Grüne Säule by Erich Reusch in front of the Staats- und Universitätsbibliothek in Göttingen, 1992

Broken Column/Gebrochene Säule by George Rickey in the park of the employment office in Dortmund, 1993

Emil Schumacher and Eckhard Gerber in conversation, 1994

is not supplemented through decoration but reflected, in its function, from a different, freer perspective. Precisely in this way, however, in the reality of later use, Gerber endows art in architecture with its perhaps most direct effect: namely, to enhance the quality of the space for those who spend time in it, and thus ultimately also to increase the identification of users with the architecture and space that surround them.

Designs by Emil Schumacher for the ceramic wall at the employment office in Dortmund, 1993

Emil Schumacher *GG-17/1993*, 1993, 38 × 53.5 cm; *GG-18/1993*, 1993, 36.5 × 49.5 cm, mixed technique on handmade paper, Emil Schumacher Museum, Hagen

Ceramic wall by Emil Schumacher,
employment office in Dortmund,
1995

Gerber Architekten and Art in Architecture

Emil Schumacher

No title, ceramic wall design, Agentur für Arbeit Dortmund (1995)

George Warren Rickey

Broken Columnn/Gebrochene Säule, sculpture, Agentur für Arbeit Dortmund (1993)

Triangles Horizontal Jointed/Dreiecke horizontal verbunden, sculpture, Agentur für Arbeit Dortmund (1995)

Cluster of Cubes/Gruppe aus vier Würfeln, Harenberg City Center, Dortmund (1991) (no longer installed)

Matt Mullican

Einhundertachtundzwanzig, hand-painted glass plates, Universität Heidelberg, Center for Integrative Infectious Disease Research (CIID)

Friedrich Meckseper

Göttinger Alphabet, glass objects, Niedersächsische Staats- und Universitätsbibliothek Göttingen (1993)

Erich Reusch

No title (*Grüne Säule*), aluminum and Anröchter dolomite, Niedersächsische Staats- und Universitätsbibliothek Göttingen (1992)

Ayse Erkmen

Namenstafel, installation, Fachhochschule Gelsenkirchen (1999)

Jürgen Weber

Windsbräute, bronze sculpture, city hall, Hagen (1984)

Eberhard Linke

Gauklerbrunnen, bronze sculptures, Stadtgarten city rail stop, Dortmund (1980•1982)

Matthäusbrücke, bronze sculpture, Bildungs- und Wissenschaftszentrum der Bundesfinanzverwaltung Münster (1982•1989)

Dortmunder Annäherung, bronze sculptures, Staatsanwaltschaft und Amtsgericht Dortmund (1998•2000)

Saltarelle, bronze sculpture, Tönnishof, Dortmund-Kley

Raffael Rheinsberg

Eine andere Generation, installation, Westfälische Hochschule Recklinghausen (2000)

Horst Linn

Landschaftstor, steel sculpture, Vechta county hall (1998)

Wall object, steel, Sparkasse Dortmund, Beratungs-Center Münsterstraße (1999)

Leucht-Turm, stainless steel pedestal, Betenhof, Dortmund (2006)

Andreas M. Kaufmann

Maschinerie für Reuleaux, light installation, TH Köln, Campus Gummersbach (2007)

Pitt Moog

Wall and ceiling paintings, Berufsschulzentrum Lüdenscheid (1977)

Column and ceiling paintings, Bildungs- und Wissenschaftszentrum der Bundesfinanzverwaltung Münster (1987)

Wall painting, Tönnishof, Dortmund-Kley

Wall and ceiling paintings, Heinz-Bach-Haus, Continentale Versicherungsverbund, Head Office, Dortmund

Hugo Kükelhaus

Wall sculpture, Sparkasse, Soest (covered up and thus not visible)

Günther Zins

Der Würfel ist gefallen, steel sculpture, customs administration, Gescherweg, Münster

Sculptures, Niedersächsisches Landesamt für Ökologie, Hildesheim; Tönnishof, Dortmund-Kley; vacation house at the Karerpass

Ekrem Yalcindag

Red, Yellow and Blue, wall design, Justus-Liebig-Universität Gießen, chemistry building (2014)

Sabine Funke

No title, wall design, Chemical and Veterinary Investigation Office MEL Münster (2002)

Aen Sauerborn

Skulptur SO 8, sculpture, Bildungs- und Wissenschaftszentrum der Bundesfinanzverwaltung Münster (1987)

Hubertus von Pilgrim

Die Laufenden, bronze sculpture, Bildungs- und Wissenschaftszentrum der Bundesfinanzverwaltung Münster (1985•1988)

Wilfried Hagebölling

Raumschneise, sculpture, Bildungs- und Wissenschaftszentrum der Bundesfinanzverwaltung Münster (1981•1987)

Vadim Kosmatschof

Die Hand, sculpture, Bildungs- und Wissenschaftszentrum der Bundesfinanzverwaltung Münster (1987)

Klaus Bönnighausen

Tor, sculpture, Bildungs- und Wissenschaftszentrum der Bundesfinanzverwaltung Münster (1987)

Source: Gerber Architekten

Authors

Prof. Dr.-Ing. Falk Jaeger Studied architecture and art history • writer, architecture critic, and architectural historian • teaching at various universities in the subjects of architectural history and architectural theory • publications on topics of contemporary architecture, the history and theory of architecture, and historical preservation

Kaspar Kraemer Architect, founder, and owner of Kaspar Kraemer Architekten BDA (KKA) • son of architect and university professor Friedrich Wilhelm Kraemer • 1998–2008, vice-president of the Bundesverband der freien Berufe BfB (Federation of German Independent Professionals) • 2001–2007, president of the Bund Deutscher Architekten (Association of German Architects, BDA) • 2007–2012, member of the advisory board of the Bundesstiftung Baukultur (Federal Foundation of Baukultur), Potsdam

Dr. phil. Gerhard Langemeyer Studied art history, classical archeology, and philosophy • director of the Museum für Kunst und Kulturgeschichte (Museum of Art and Cultural History) in Dortmund • since 1986, head of cultural affairs, 1995, treasurer and city manager of Dortmund • 1999–2009, mayor of Dortmund (during his tenure: flagship projects such as library, concert hall, Dortmunder U, and the urban redevelopment of the PHOENIX area)

Rouven Lotz Art historian, museum director, and curator • studied art history and comparative textile sciences • since 2011, scientific director of the Emil Schumacher Museum in Hagen • since 2009, managing director of the Henry van de Velde Gesellschaft (Henry van de Velde Society) • curator of exhibitions on Emil Schumacher, Karel Appel, Henri de Toulouse-Lautrec, and others • publications on twentieth-century art

Sebastian Redecke Studied architecture at TU Braunschweig and the University of Rome • editor of the journal *Bauwelt* in Berlin • member of numerous juries

Prof. Dipl.-Ing. Christa Reicher Architect and urban planner • since October 2018, holder of the Chair for Urban Planning and Design and director of the Institute for Urban Planning and European Urban Studies at the Faculty of Architecture of RWTH Aachen • partner of the planning office RHA, which she co-founded

Dr. h. c. Dietrich E. Sattler Studied book design • editor of the Frankfurt Hölderlin edition (Roter Stern, today Stroemfeld) • a friend of Eckhard Gerber since their childhood in Thuringia • from 1978 until his retirement, research assistant at the Universität Bremen (University of Bremen) • founder of the publishing house Neue Bremer Presse, where he published the twenty-two-volume *Bremer Bibel* (Bremen Bible), among other things • honorary doctorate from the Universität Hamburg (University of Hamburg)

Prof. Dr. Wolfgang Sonne Studied art history and classical archeology • since 2007, professor of history and theory of architecture at TU Dortmund • scientific director of the Baukunstarchiv NRW (Architectural Archive of North Rhine-Westphalia) • deputy director of the Deutsches Institut für Stadtbaukunst (German Institute for Urban Planning) • research focus: architecture and urban planning from the nineteenth to twenty-first century

Prof. Jörn Walter Studied spatial planning • 1999–2017, chief planning director of the Free and Hanseatic City of Hamburg • played a decisive role in urban planning in Hamburg, especially with the HafenCity • lectureships in Vienna and Dresden • since 2014, honorary professor at HafenCity Universität Hamburg (HafenCity University Hamburg) • member of the Akademie der Künste (Academy of Arts) in Berlin, Saxony, and Hamburg

Picture Credits

Hans Blossey p. 122 • Andreas Bormann p. 49 • *Braunschweiger Zeitung*, Steffens p. 62 top, 65 • Marcus Bredt p. 13 • Eric Brown p. 95 • Marliese Darsow p. 106 bottom, 107, 243 • Emil Schumacher: VG Bild-Kunst, Bonn 2019 p. 239 bottom, 249 • euroluftbild. de/Swissphoto GmbH/Uwe Lange p. 116 bottom • Framepool RS GmbH p. 116 top • Gerber Architekten p. 17, 19 middle, 19 bottom, 20, 21, 23, 27 bottom, 31 top, 32, 35, 38, 43, 46, 62 bottom, 63, 66, 70, 135 bottom, 74, 75, 80 middle, 80 bottom, 89 middle, 89 bottom, 119, 142 top, 147 bottom, 157, 163, 168, 169, 170, 172, 176, 178, 179, 180 bottom, 186, 246 top, 247 bottom • Heinrich Heidersberger, #937_15 Landtag Niedersachsen, Hannover 1962, Institut Heidersberger, www.heidersberger.de p. 54 top • Heinrich Heidersberger, #942_1 Model Zwölf-Apostel-Kirche, Hildesheim 1963, Institut Heidersberger, www.heidersberger.de p. 54 middle • Heinrich Heidersberger, #9025_3 Portrait Friedrich Wilhelm Kraemer 1954, Institut Heidersberger, www.heidersberger.de p. 52 right • Heinrich Heidersberger, #807_39 Unterharzer Hüttenwerke, Goslar 1959, Institut Heidersberger, www.heidersberger.de p. 57 • HG Esch p. 87, 111 bottom, 127 bottom, 142 bottom • Christian Jochheim p. 247 • Manfred Kaddik p. 31 bottom MDR Landesfunkhaus Sachsen-Anhalt, Magdeburg p. 186 top • Taufik Kenan p. 180 top • KONGRESS- und EVENTPARK, Stadthalle Hagen GmbH p. 239 top • Hans Jürgen Landes p. 14, 86, 90, 97, 128 bottom, 133, 134 top, 141, 147 top, 151, 182, 183, 184, 185, 186 bottom, 250, 251 • Heiner Leiska p. 131, 160 • Dieter Leistner p. 101 bottom, 106 top, 153 • Metilsteiner, Lizenz_Creative Commons p. 27 top • Oskar C. Neubauer p. 148 bottom • Dieter Oesterlen, *Bauten und Texte*, Berlin 1995, P. 7 p. 52 left • Klemens Ortmeyer p. 147 top, 154 • Irene Osei-Poku p. 188, 189 • Picasa, Lizenz_Creative Commons, Editor: Gerber Architekten p. 19 top • Christian Richters p. 137, 140, 152 top, 162, 165, 173, 174, 175, 244 top, 246 top • Walter Schulte p. 83, 89 top, 128 top • Philipp Stoltz p. 54 bottom • Friedrich Thomas p. 72 top • Tönnis p. 126 • Peter Walser p. 91, 94, 95 bottom, 102, 111 top, 101 top, 127, 244 bottom • Werkgemeinschaft 66 p. 78, 80 top, 84, 96, 98 • *Westfalenpost*, no. 57 p. 72 bottom

Cover based on a design by Amir Rezaloo | RBfK

Editors: Dieter Nellen and Jürgen Tietz
Editorial Team: Soudabeh Khan, Sabine Weicherding, and Gesche Gerber, Gerber Architekten
Translation: Michael Thomas Taylor, Berlin
Copy Editor: Benjamin R. Trivers, Berlin
Setting: Daniela Mecklenburg, Iffeldorf
Lithography: Bild1Druck, Berlin
Printed in the European Union

Bibliographic information published by the Deutsche Nationalbibliothek
The Deutsche Nationalbibliothek lists this publication in the Deutsche Nationalbibliografie;
detailed bibliographic data are available on the Internet at http://dnb.d-nb.de

jovis Verlag GmbH
Kurfürstenstraße 15/16
10785 Berlin

www.jovis.de

jovis books are available worldwide in select bookstores. Please contact your nearest bookseller or visit www.jovis.de for information concerning your local distribution.

ISBN 978-3-86859-500-0